VGM Professional Resumes Series

SECOND EDITION

RESUMES FOR

PERFORMING ARTS CAREERS

With Sample Cover Letters

The Editors of VGM Career Books

McGraw-Hill

New York   Chicago   San Francisco   Lisbon   London   Madrid   Mexico City
Milan   New Delhi   San Juan   Seoul   Singapore   Sydney   Toronto

Library of Congress Cataloging-in-Publication Data

Resumes for performing arts careers / the editors of VGM Career Books.—2nd ed.
    p.   cm. — (VGM professional resumes series)
    ISBN 0-07-141162-3
    1. Performing arts—Vocational guidance—United States   2. Resumes
(Employment)   I. VGM Career Books (Firm)   II. Series.

PN1580.R47   2004
791'.023'73—dc22   2003025819

1 2 3 4 5 6 7 8 9 0   QPD/QPD   3 2 1 0 9 8 7 6 5 4

ISBN 0-07-141162-3

McGraw-Hill books are available at special quantity discounts to use as premiums and sales
promotions, or for use in corporate training programs. For more information, please write to
the Director of Special Sales, Professional Publishing, McGraw-Hill, Two Penn Plaza, New
York, NY 10121-2298. Or contact your local bookstore.

This book is printed on acid-free paper.

Contents

Introduction

Your resume is a piece of paper (or an electronic document) that serves to introduce you to the people who will eventually hire you. To write a thoughtful resume, you must thoroughly assess your personality, your accomplishments, and the skills you have acquired. The act of composing and submitting a resume also requires you to carefully consider the company or individual that might hire you. What are they looking for, and how can you meet their needs? This book shows you how to organize your personal information and experience into a concise and well-written resume so that your qualifications and potential as an employee will be understood easily and quickly by a complete stranger.

Writing the resume is just one step in what can be a daunting job-search process, but it is an important element in the chain of events that will lead you to your new position. While you are probably a talented, bright, and charming person, your resume may not reflect these qualities. A poorly written resume can get you nowhere; a well-written resume can land you an interview and potentially a job. A good resume can even lead the interviewer to ask you questions that will allow you to talk about your strengths and highlight the skills you can bring to a prospective employer. Even a person with very little experience can find a good job if he or she is assisted by a thoughtful and polished resume.

Lengthy, typewritten resumes are a thing of the past. Today, employers do not have the time or the patience for verbose documents; they look for tightly composed, straightforward, action-based resumes. Although a one-page resume is the norm, a two-page resume may be warranted if you have had extensive job experience or have changed careers and truly need the space to properly position yourself. If, after careful editing, you still need more than one page to present yourself, it's acceptable to use a second page. A crowded resume that's hard to read would be the worst of your choices.

Distilling your work experience, education, and interests into such a small space requires preparation and thought. This book takes you step-by-step through the process of crafting an effective resume that will stand out in today's competitive marketplace. It serves as a workbook and a place to write down your experiences, while also including the techniques you'll need to pull all the necessary elements together. In the following pages, you'll find many examples of resumes that are specific to your area of interest. Study them for inspiration and find what appeals to you. There are a variety of ways to organize and present your information; inside, you'll find several that will be suitable to your needs. Good luck landing the job of your dreams!

The Elements of an Effective Resume

An effective resume is composed of information that employers are most interested in knowing about a prospective job applicant. This information is conveyed by a few essential elements. The following is a list of elements that are found in most resumes—some essential, some optional. Later in this chapter, we will further examine the role of each of these elements in the makeup of your resume.

- Heading

- Objective and/or Keyword Section

- Work Experience

- Education

- Honors

- Activities

- Certificates and Licenses

- Publications

- Professional Memberships

- Special Skills

- Personal Information

- References

The first step in preparing your resume is to gather information about yourself and your past accomplishments. Later you will refine this information, rewrite it using effective language, and organize it into an attractive layout. But first, let's take a look at each of these important elements individually so you can judge their appropriateness for your resume.

Heading

Although the heading may seem to be the simplest section of your resume, be careful not to take it lightly. It is the first section your prospective employer will see, and it contains the information she or he will need to contact you. At the very least, the heading must contain your name, your home address, and, of course, a phone number where you can be reached easily.

In today's high-tech world, many of us have multiple ways that we can be contacted. You may list your e-mail address if you are reasonably sure the employer makes use of this form of communication. Keep in mind, however, that others may have access to your e-mail messages if you send them from an account provided by your current company. If this is a concern, do not list your work e-mail address on your resume. If you are able to take calls at your current place of business, you should include your work number, because most employers will attempt to contact you during typical business hours.

If you have voice mail or a reliable answering machine at home or at work, list its number in the heading and make sure your greeting is professional and clear. Always include at least one phone number in your heading, even if it is a temporary number, where a prospective employer can leave a message.

You might have a dozen different ways to be contacted, but you do not need to list all of them. Confine your numbers or addresses to those that are the easiest for the prospective employer to use and the simplest for you to retrieve.

Objective

When seeking a specific career path, it is important to list a job or career objective on your resume. This statement helps employers know the direction you see yourself taking, so they can determine whether your goals are in line with those of their organization and the position available. Normally, an objective is one to two sentences long. Its contents will vary depending on your career field, goals, and personality. The objective can be specific or general, but it should always be to the point. See the sample resumes in this book for examples.

If you are planning to use this resume online, or you suspect your potential employer is likely to scan your resume, you will want to include a "keyword" in the objective. This allows a prospective employer, searching hundreds of resumes for a specific skill or position objective, to locate the keyword and find your resume. In essence, a keyword is what's "hot" in your particular field at a given time. It's a buzzword, a shorthand way of getting a particular message across at a glance. For example, if you are a lawyer, your objective might state your desire to work in the area of corporate litigation. In this case, someone searching for the keyword "corporate litigation" will pull up your resume and know that you want to plan, research, and present cases at trial on behalf of the corporation. If your objective states that you "desire a challenging position in systems design," the keyword is "systems design," an industry-specific shorthand way of saying that you want to be involved in assessing the need for, acquiring, and implementing high-technology systems. These are keywords and every industry has them, so it's becoming more and more important to include a few in your resume. (You may need to conduct additional research to make sure you know what keywords are most likely to be used in your desired industry, profession, or situation.)

There are many resume and job-search sites online. Like most things in the online world, they vary a great deal in quality. Use your discretion. If you plan to apply for jobs online or advertise your availability this way, you will want to design a scannable resume. This type of resume uses a format that can be easily scanned into a computer and added to a database. Scanning allows a prospective employer to use keywords to quickly review each applicant's experience and skills, and (in the event that there are many candidates for the job) to keep your resume for future reference.

Many people find that it is worthwhile to create two or more versions of their basic resume. You may want an intricately designed resume on high-quality paper to mail or hand out *and* a resume that is designed to be scanned into a computer and saved on a database or an online job site. You can even create a resume in ASCII text to e-mail to prospective employers. For further information, you may wish to refer to the *Guide to Internet Job Searching*, by Frances Roehm and Margaret Dikel, updated and published every other year by VGM Career Books, a division of the McGraw-Hill Companies. This excellent book contains helpful and detailed information about formatting a resume for Internet use. To get you started, in Chapter 3 we have included a list of things to keep in mind when creating electronic resumes.

Although it is usually a good idea to include an objective, in some cases this element is not necessary. The goal of the objective statement is to provide the employer with an idea of where you see yourself going in the field. However, if you are uncertain of the exact nature of the job you seek, including an objective that is too specific could result in your not being considered for a host of perfectly acceptable positions. If you decide not to use an objective heading in your resume, you should definitely incorporate the information that would be conveyed in the objective into your cover letter.

Work Experience

Work experience is arguably the most important element of them all. Unless you are a recent graduate or former homemaker with little or no relevant work experience, your current and former positions will provide the central focus of the resume. You will want this section to be as complete and carefully constructed as possible. By thoroughly examining your work experience, you can get to the heart of your accomplishments and present them in a way that demonstrates and highlights your qualifications.

If you are just entering the workforce, your resume will probably focus on your education, but you should also include information on your work or volunteer experiences. Although you will have less information about work experience than a person who has held multiple positions or is advanced in his or her career, the amount of information is not what is most important in this section. How the information is presented and what it says about you as a worker and a person are what really count.

As you create this section of your resume, remember the need for accuracy. Include all the necessary information about each of your jobs, including your job title, dates of employment, name of your employer, city, state, responsibilities, special projects you handled, and accomplishments. Be sure to list only accomplishments for which you were directly responsible. And don't be alarmed if you haven't participated in or worked on special projects, because this section may not be relevant to certain jobs.

The most common way to list your work experience is in *reverse chronological order*. In other words, start with your most recent job and work your way backward. This way, your prospective employer sees your current (and often most important) position before considering your past employment. Your most recent position, if it's the most important in terms of responsibilities and relevance to the job for which you are applying, should also be the one that includes the most information as compared to your previous positions.

Even if the work itself seems unrelated to your proposed career path, you should list any job or experience that will help sell your talents. If you were promoted or given greater responsibilities or commendations, be sure to mention the fact.

The following worksheet is provided to help you organize your experiences in the working world. It will also serve as an excellent resource to refer to when updating your resume in the future.

WORK EXPERIENCE

Job One:

Job Title _____

Dates _____

Employer _____

City, State _____

Major Duties _____

_____

_____

_____

_____

_____

_____

_____

_____

Special Projects _____

_____

_____

_____

Accomplishments _____

_____

_____

_____

_____

_____

Job Two:

Job Title _____

Dates _____

Employer _____

City, State _____

Major Duties _____

_____

_____

_____

_____

_____

_____

Special Projects _____

_____

_____

Accomplishments _____

_____

_____

_____

_____

_____

_____

_____

Job Three:

Job Title _____

Dates _____

Employer _____

City, State _____

Major Duties _____

_____

_____

_____

_____

_____

_____

Special Projects _____

_____

_____

_____

Accomplishments _____

_____

_____

_____

_____

_____

_____

_____

Job Four:

Job Title _____

Dates _____

Employer _____

City, State _____

Major Duties _____

_____

_____

_____

_____

_____

_____

_____

_____

Special Projects _____

_____

_____

_____

Accomplishments _____

_____

_____

_____

_____

_____

_____

_____

Education

Education is usually the second most important element of a resume. Your educational background is often a deciding factor in an employer's decision to interview you. Highlight your accomplishments in school as much as you did those accomplishments at work. If you are looking for your first professional job, your education or life experience will be your greatest asset because your related work experience will be minimal. In this case, the education section becomes the most important means of selling yourself.

Include in this section all the degrees or certificates you have received; your major or area of concentration; all of the honors you earned; and any relevant activities you participated in, organized, or chaired. Again, list your most recent schooling first. If you have completed graduate-level work, begin with that and work your way back through your undergraduate education. If you have completed college, you generally should not list your high school experience; do so only if you earned special honors, you had a grade point average that was much better than the norm, or this was your highest level of education.

If you have completed a large number of credit hours in a subject that may be relevant to the position you are seeking but did not obtain a degree, you may wish to list the hours or classes you completed. Keep in mind, however, that you may be asked to explain why you did not finish the program. If you are currently in school, list the degree, certificate, or license you expect to obtain and the projected date of completion.

The following worksheet will help you gather the information you need for this section of your resume.

EDUCATION

School One _____

Major or Area of Concentration _____

Degree _____

Dates _____

School Two _____

Major or Area of Concentration _____

Degree _____

Dates _____

Honors

If you include an honors section in your resume, you should highlight any awards, honors, or memberships in honorary societies that you have received. (You may also incorporate this information into your education section.) Often, the honors are academic in nature, but this section also may be used for special achievements in sports, clubs, or other school activities. Always include the name of the organization awarding the honor and the date(s) received. Use the following worksheet to help you gather your information.

HONORS

Honor One _____

Awarding Organization _____

Date(s) _____

Honor Two _____

Awarding Organization _____

Date(s) _____

Honor Three _____

Awarding Organization _____

Date(s) _____

Honor Four _____

Awarding Organization _____

Date(s) _____

Honor Five _____

Awarding Organization _____

Date(s) _____

Activities

Perhaps you have been active in different organizations or clubs; often an employer will look at such involvement as evidence of initiative, dedication, and good social skills. Examples of your ability to take a leading role in a group should be included on a resume, if you can provide them. The activities section of your resume should present neighborhood and community activities, volunteer positions, and so forth. In general, you may want to avoid listing any organization whose name indicates the race, creed, sex, age, marital status, sexual orientation, or nation of origin of its members because this could expose you to discrimination. Use the following worksheet to list the specifics of your activities.

ACTIVITIES

Organization/Activity _____

Accomplishments _____

_____

_____

Organization/Activity _____

Accomplishments _____

_____

_____

Organization/Activity _____

Accomplishments _____

_____

_____

As your work experience grows through the years, your school activities and honors will carry less weight and be emphasized less in your resume. Eventually, you will probably list only your degree and any major honors received. As time goes by, your job performance and the experience you've gained become the most important elements in your resume, which should change to reflect this.

Certificates and Licenses

If your chosen career path requires specialized training, you may already have certificates or licenses. You should list these if the job you are seeking requires them and you, of course, have acquired them. If you have applied for a license but have not yet received it, use the phrase "application pending."

License requirements vary by state. If you have moved or are planning to relocate to another state, check with that state's board or licensing agency for all licensing requirements.

Always make sure that all of the information you list is completely accurate. Locate copies of your certificates and licenses, and check the exact date and name of the accrediting agency. Use the following worksheet to organize the necessary information.

CERTIFICATES AND LICENSES

Name of License _____

Licensing Agency _____

Date Issued _____

Name of License _____

Licensing Agency _____

Date Issued _____

Name of License _____

Licensing Agency _____

Date Issued _____

Publications

Some professions strongly encourage or even require that you publish. If you have written, coauthored, or edited any books, articles, professional papers, or works of a similar nature that pertain to your field, you will definitely want to include this element. Remember to list the date of publication and the publisher's name, and specify whether you were the sole author or a coauthor. Book, magazine, or journal titles are generally italicized, while the titles of articles within a larger publication appear in quotes. (Check with your reference librarian for more about the appropriate way to present this information.) For scientific or research papers, you will need to give the date, place, and audience to whom the paper was presented.

Use the following worksheet to help you gather the necessary information about your publications.

PUBLICATIONS

Title and Type (Note, Article, etc.) _____

Title of Publication (Journal, Book, etc.) _____

Publisher _____

Date Published _____

Title and Type (Note, Article, etc.) _____

Title of Publication (Journal, Book, etc.) _____

Publisher _____

Date Published _____

Title and Type (Note, Article, etc.) _____

Title of Publication (Journal, Book, etc.) _____

Publisher _____

Date Published _____

Professional Memberships

Another potential element in your resume is a section listing professional memberships. Use this section to describe your involvement in professional associations, unions, and similar organizations. It is to your advantage to list any professional memberships that pertain to the job you are seeking. Many employers see your membership as representative of your desire to stay up-to-date and connected in your field. Include the dates of your involvement and whether you took part in any special activities or held any offices within the organization. Use the following worksheet to organize your information.

PROFESSIONAL MEMBERSHIPS

Name of Organization _____

Office(s) Held _____

Activities _____

Dates _____

Name of Organization _____

Office(s) Held _____

Activities _____

Dates _____

Name of Organization _____

Office(s) Held _____

Activities _____

Dates _____

Name of Organization _____

Office(s) Held _____

Activities _____

Dates _____

Special Skills

The special skills section of your resume is the place to mention any special abilities you have that relate to the job you are seeking. You can use this element to present certain talents or experiences that are not necessarily a part of your education or work experience. Common examples include fluency in a foreign language, extensive travel abroad, or knowledge of a particular computer application. "Special skills" can encompass a wide range of talents, and this section can be used creatively. However, for each skill you list, you should be able to describe how it would be a direct asset in the type of work you're seeking because employers may ask just that in an interview. If you can't think of a way to do this, it may be extraneous information.

Personal Information

Some people include personal information on their resumes. This is generally not recommended, but you might wish to include it if you think that something in your personal life, such as a hobby or talent, has some bearing on the position you are seeking. This type of information is often referred to at the beginning of an interview, when it may be used as an icebreaker. Of course, personal information regarding your age, marital status, race, religion, or sexual orientation should never appear on your resume as personal information. It should be given only in the context of memberships and activities, and only when doing so would not expose you to discrimination.

References

References are not usually given on the resume itself, but a prospective employer needs to know that you have references who may be contacted if necessary. All you need to include is a single sentence at the end of the resume: "References are available upon request," or even simply, "References available." Have a reference list ready—your interviewer may ask to see it! Contact each person on the list ahead of time to see whether it is all right for you to use him or her as a reference. This way, the person has a chance to think about what to say *before* the call occurs. This helps ensure that you will obtain the best reference possible.

Chapter 2

Writing Your Resume

Now that you have gathered the information for each section of your resume, it's time to write it out in a way that will get the attention of the reviewer—hopefully, your future employer! The language you use in your resume will affect its success, so you must be careful and conscientious. Translate the facts you have gathered into the active, precise language of resume writing. You will be aiming for a resume that keeps the reader's interest and highlights your accomplishments in a concise and effective way.

Resume writing is unlike any other form of writing. Although your seventh-grade composition teacher would not approve, the rules of punctuation and sentence building are often completely ignored. Instead, you should try for a functional, direct writing style that focuses on the use of verbs and other words that imply action on your part. Writing with action words and strong verbs characterizes you to potential employers as an energetic, active person, someone who completes tasks and achieves results from his or her work. Resumes that do not make use of action words can sound passive and stale. These resumes are not effective and do not get the attention of any employer, no matter how qualified the applicant. Choose words that display your strengths and demonstrate your initiative. The following list of commonly used verbs will help you create a strong resume:

administered	assembled
advised	assumed responsibility
analyzed	billed
arranged	built

carried out

channeled

collected

communicated

compiled

completed

conducted

contacted

contracted

coordinated

counseled

created

cut

designed

determined

developed

directed

dispatched

distributed

documented

edited

established

expanded

functioned as

gathered

handled

hired

implemented

improved

inspected

interviewed

introduced

invented

maintained

managed

met with

motivated

negotiated

operated

orchestrated

ordered

organized

oversaw

performed

planned

prepared

presented

produced

programmed

published

purchased

recommended

recorded

reduced

referred

represented

researched

reviewed

saved	supervised
screened	taught
served as	tested
served on	trained
sold	typed
suggested	wrote

Let's look at two examples that differ only in their writing style. The first resume section is ineffective because it does not use action words to accent the applicant's work experiences.

WORK EXPERIENCE
Regional Sales Manager

Manager of sales representatives from seven states. Manager of twelve food chain accounts in the East. In charge of the sales force's planned selling toward specific goals. Supervisor and trainer of new sales representatives. Consulting for customers in the areas of inventory management and quality control.

Special Projects: Coordinator and sponsor of annual food-industry sales seminar.

Accomplishments: Monthly regional volume went up 25 percent during my tenure while, at the same time, a proper sales/cost ratio was maintained. Customer-company relations were improved.

In the following paragraph, we have rewritten the same section using action words. Notice how the tone has changed. It now sounds stronger and more active. This person accomplished goals and really *did* things.

WORK EXPERIENCE
Regional Sales Manager

Managed sales representatives from seven states. Oversaw twelve food chain accounts in the eastern United States. Directed the sales force in planned selling toward specific goals. Supervised and trained new sales representatives. Counseled customers in the areas of inventory management and quality control. Coordinated and sponsored the annual Food Industry Seminar. Increased monthly regional volume by 25 percent and helped to improve customer-company relations during my tenure.

One helpful way to construct the work experience section is to make use of your actual job descriptions—the written duties and expectations your employers had for a person in your current or former position. Job descriptions are rarely written in proper resume language, so you will have to rework them, but they do include much of the information necessary to create this section of your resume. If you have access to job descriptions for your former positions, you can use the details to construct an action-oriented paragraph. Often, your human resources department can provide a job description for your current position.

The following is an example of a typical human resources job description, followed by a rewritten version of the same description employing action words and specific details about the job. Again, pay attention to the style of writing instead of the content, as the details of your own experience will be unique.

WORK EXPERIENCE
Public Administrator I

Responsibilities: Coordinate and direct public services to meet the needs of the nation, state, or community. Analyze problems; work with special committees and public agencies; recommend solutions to governing bodies.

Aptitudes and Skills: Ability to relate to and communicate with people; solve complex problems through analysis; plan, organize, and implement policies and programs. Knowledge of political systems, financial management, personnel administration, program evaluation, and organizational theory.

WORK EXPERIENCE
Public Administrator I

Wrote pamphlets and conducted discussion groups to inform citizens of legislative processes and consumer issues. Organized and supervised 25 interviewers. Trained interviewers in effective communication skills.

After you have written out your resume, you are ready to begin the next important step: assembly and layout.

Chapter 3

Assembly and Layout

At this point, you've gathered all the necessary information for your resume and rewritten it in language that will impress your potential employers. Your next step is to assemble the sections in a logical order and lay them out on the page neatly and attractively to achieve the desired effect: getting the interview.

Assembly

The order of the elements in a resume makes a difference in its overall effect. Clearly, you would not want to bury your name and address somewhere in the middle of the resume. Nor would you want to lead with a less important section, such as special skills. Put the elements in an order that stresses your most important accomplishments and the things that will be most appealing to your potential employer. For example, if you are new to the workforce, you will want the reviewer to read about your education and life skills before any part-time jobs you may have held for short durations. On the other hand, if you have been gainfully employed for several years and currently hold an important position in your company, you should list your work accomplishments ahead of your educational information, which has become less pertinent with time.

Certain things should always be included in your resume, but others are optional. The following list shows you which are which. You might want to use it as a checklist to be certain that you have included all of the necessary information.

Essential	Optional
Name	Cellular Phone Number
Address	Pager Number
Phone Number	E-Mail Address or Website Address
Work Experience	Voice Mail Number
Education	Job Objective
References Phrase	Honors
	Special Skills
	Publications
	Professional Memberships
	Activities
	Certificates and Licenses
	Personal Information
	Graphics
	Photograph

Your choice of optional sections depends on your own background and employment needs. Always use information that will put you in a favorable light—unless it's absolutely essential, avoid anything that will prompt the interviewer to ask questions about your weaknesses or something else that could be unflattering. Make sure your information is accurate and truthful. If your honors are impressive, include them in the resume. If your activities in school demonstrate talents that are necessary for the job you are seeking, allow space for a section on activities. If you are applying for a position that requires ornamental illustration, you may want to include border illustrations or graphics that demonstrate your talents in this area. If you are answering an advertisement for a job that requires certain physical traits, a photo of yourself might be appropriate. A person applying for a job as a computer programmer would *not* include a photo as part of his or her resume. Each resume is unique, just as each person is unique.

Types of Resumes

So far we have focused on the most common type of resume—the *reverse chronological* resume—in which your most recent job is listed first. This is the type of resume usually preferred by those who have to read a large number of resumes, and it is by far the most popular and widely circulated. However, this style of presentation may not be the most effective way to highlight *your* skills and accomplishments.

For example, if you are reentering the workforce after many years or are trying to change career fields, the *functional* resume may work best. This type of resume puts the focus on your achievements instead of the sequence of your work history. In the functional resume, your experience is presented through your general accomplishments and the skills you have developed in your working life.

A functional resume is assembled from the same information you gathered in Chapter 1. The main difference lies in how you organize the information. Essentially, the work experience section is divided in two, with your job duties and accomplishments constituting one section and your employers' names, cities, and states; your positions; and the dates employed making up the other. Place the first section near the top of your resume, just below your job objective (if used), and call it *Accomplishments* or *Achievements*. The second section, containing the bare essentials of your work history, should come after the accomplishments section and can be called *Employment History*, since it is a chronological overview of your former jobs.

The other sections of your resume remain the same. The work experience section is the only one affected in the functional format. By placing the section that focuses on your achievements at the beginning, you draw attention to these achievements. This puts less emphasis on where you worked and when, and more on what you did and what you are capable of doing.

If you are changing careers, the emphasis on skills and achievements is important. The identities of previous employers (who aren't part of your new career field) need to be downplayed. A functional resume can help accomplish this task. If you are reentering the workforce after a long absence, a functional resume is the obvious choice. And if you lack full-time work experience, you will need to draw attention away from this fact and put the focus on your skills and abilities. You may need to highlight your volunteer activities and part-time work. Education may also play a more important role in your resume.

The type of resume that is right for you will depend on your personal circumstances. It may be helpful to create both types and then compare them. Which one presents you in the best light? Examples of both types of resumes are included in this book. Use the sample resumes in Chapter 5 to help you decide on the content, presentation, and look of your own resume.

Resume or Curriculum Vitae?

A curriculum vitae (CV) is a longer, more detailed synopsis of your professional history, which generally runs three or more pages in length. It includes a summary of your educational and academic background as well as teaching and research experience, publications, presentations, awards, honors, affiliations, and other details. Because the purpose of the CV is different from that of the resume, many of the rules we've discussed thus far involving style and length do not apply.

A curriculum vitae is used primarily for admissions applications to graduate or professional schools, independent consulting in a variety of settings, proposals for fellowships or grants, or applications for positions in academia. As with a resume, you may need different versions of a CV for different types of positions. You should only send a CV when one is specifically requested by an employer or institution.

Like a resume, your CV should include your name, contact information, education, skills, and experience. In addition to the basics, a CV includes research and teaching experience, publications, grants and fellowships, professional associations and licenses, awards, and other information relevant to the position for which you are applying. You can follow the advice presented thus far to gather and organize your personal information.

Special Tips for Electronic Resumes

Because there are many details to consider in writing a resume that will be posted or transmitted on the Internet, or one that will be scanned into a computer when it is received, we suggest that you refer to the *Guide to Internet Job Searching*, by Frances Roehm and Margaret Dikel, as previously mentioned. However, here are some brief, general guidelines to follow if you expect your resume to be scanned into a computer.

- Use standard fonts in which none of the letters touch.

- Keep in mind that underlining, italics, and fancy scripts may not scan well.

- Use boldface and capitalization to set off elements. Again, make sure letters don't touch. Leave at least a quarter inch between lines of type.

- Keep information and elements at the left margin. Centering, columns, and even indenting may change when the resume is optically scanned.

- Do not use any lines, boxes, or graphics.

- Place the most important information at the top of the first page. If you use two pages, put "Page 1 of 2" at the bottom of the first page and put your name and "Page 2 of 2" at the top of the second page.

- List each telephone number on its own line in the header.

- Use multiple keywords or synonyms for what you do to make sure your qualifications will be picked up if a prospective employer is searching for them. Use nouns that are keywords for your profession.

- Be descriptive in your titles. For example, don't just use "assistant"; use "legal office assistant."

- Make sure the contrast between print and paper is good. Use a high-quality laser printer and white or very light colored 8½-by-11-inch paper.

- Mail a high-quality laser print or an excellent copy. Do not fold or use staples, as this might interfere with scanning. You may, however, use paper clips.

In addition to creating a resume that works well for scanning, you may want to have a resume that can be e-mailed to reviewers. Because you may not know what word processing application the recipient uses, the best format to use is ASCII text. (ASCII stands for "American Standard Code for Information Exchange.") It allows people with very different software platforms to exchange and understand information. (E-mail operates on this principle.) ASCII is a simple, text-only language, which means you can include only simple text. There can be no use of boldface, italics, or even paragraph indentations.

To create an ASCII resume, just use your normal word processing program; when finished, save it as a "text only" document. You will find this option under the "save" or "save as" command. Here is a list of things to *avoid* when crafting your electronic resume:

- Tabs. Use your space bar. Tabs will not work.

- Any special characters, such as mathematical symbols.

- Word wrap. Use hard returns (the return key) to make line breaks.

- Centering or other formatting. Align everything at the left margin.

- Bold or italic fonts. Everything will be converted to plain text when you save the file as a "text only" document.

Check carefully for any mistakes before you save the document as a text file. Spellcheck and proofread it several times; then ask someone with a keen eye to go over it again for you. Remember: the key is to keep it simple. Any attempt to make this resume pretty or decorative may result in a resume that is confusing and hard to read. After you have saved the document, you can cut and paste it into an e-mail or onto a website.

Layout for a Paper Resume

A great deal of care—and much more formatting—is necessary to achieve an attractive layout for your paper resume. There is no single appropriate layout that applies to every resume, but there are a few basic rules to follow in putting your resume on paper:

- Leave a comfortable margin on the sides, top, and bottom of the page (usually one to one and a half inches).

- Use appropriate spacing between the sections (two to three line spaces are usually adequate).

- Be consistent in the *type* of headings you use for different sections of your resume. For example, if you capitalize the heading EMPLOY-MENT HISTORY, don't use initial capitals and underlining for a section of equal importance, such as Education.

- Do not use more than one font in your resume. Stay consistent by choosing a font that is fairly standard and easy to read, and don't change it for different sections. Beware of the tendency to try to make your resume original by choosing fancy type styles; your resume may end up looking unprofessional instead of creative. Unless you are in a very creative and artistic field, you should almost always stick with tried-and-true type styles like Times New Roman and Palatino, which are often used in business writing. In the area of resume styles, conservative is usually the best way to go.

CHRONOLOGICAL RESUME

CHRISTINA LORCA

609 Kirwan Avenue • Newton, MA 02125
(508) 555-4382 • C.Lorca@xxx.com

Education

Bachelor of Fine Arts, Dance, 2002
University of Vermont, Alpine Ridge, VT

Honors/Awards

Academic and Talent Scholarships, 1998–2002
Alpine National Honor Society
Dean's List

Dance Experience

2002	Falmouth Festival of Music and Art, Francine Denk
	Excerpts from *Barcarole*, Jared Lima
	Dances of Pearl, Elizabeth Karrol
	Golden Slumbers, Nana Lin-Hong, Reconstructed by Tani Arroyo
2001	Suite from *Hallowed Eve*, Jared Lima
	Heart of Hearts, Susan Nitz
	Dream in Red, Tani Arroyo
2000	*Lady Sings the Blues*, Rena Hartman
	Gyroscope, George Lu
	Synergetic Moments, George Lu
1993–1997	Lin-Hong Dance Company, Morrisville, VT – Director, Nana Lin-Hong

Teaching Experience

2002–present	New England School of Dance, Brockton, MA – Director, Jane Howard. Ballet, Jazz, and Tap for children ages 6 to 14.
1997–1999	Alpine Ridge Dance Center, Alpine Ridge, VT – Director, Kristi Buell. Contemporary, Creative Movement, and "Baby Steps" for toddlers and children ages 3 to 13.

Page 1 of 2

Choreographic Experience

2001	*A Rose Touched by the Sun*
	Navajo Windsong, Co-choreographed with Rebecca Sherman
2000	*Donovan's Dream*

Forms Studied

Ballet, Pointe, Jazz, Tap, Character, Modern/Contemporary, Improvisation, Pom-Pons, Synchronized Swimming

Teachers

Jared Lima, Tani Arroyo, George Lu, Rena Hartman, Cynthia Beckett, Kristi Buell, Allen Bounty, Elizabeth Karrol, Darin Alton, Nana Lin-Hong

Other Experience

New Hampshire Summer Arts Program, West Newton, NH
American Student Dance Conference, Middlebury, CT
Alpine Ridge Summer Dance Workshops, Alpine Ridge, VT

References

Jared Lima
c/o University of Vermont
Wagner Hall, School of Dance
Alpine Ridge, VT 05708

Rena Hartman
c/o University of Vermont
Wagner Hall, School of Dance
Alpine Ridge, VT 05708
R.Hartman@xxx.com

Nana Lin-Hong
Director, Lin-Hong Dance Company
11 Thompson Street
Morrisville, VT 05722

FUNCTIONAL RESUME

James Rayburn
Baritone
432 E. 55th St.
New York, NY 10011
(212) 555-2465

6′2″, 220 lbs.
Light brown hair, green eyes

Opera Performance
Schaunard, *La Boheme*	Indiana University Opera
Papageno, *The Magic Flute*	Indiana University Opera
Dancaïre, *Carmen*	Hammond Symphony
Riff, *West Side Story*	New Horizons Theater

Roles Prepared
Figaro, *Le Nozze di Figaro*
Valentin, *Faust*
Harlequin, *Ariadne auf Naxos* (German and English)

Awards
Bel Canto Foundation Competition	Second Place Winner
Metropolitan Opera Competition	Regional Finalist
NATS Competition	First Place Winner

Education
Indiana University, Bachelor of Music, 2000
Tanglewood Festival, Fellowship Recipient, 2001

Major Teachers: Franz Heidleberg, Mariana Petro, James Morrison Eady
Master Classes: Thomas Garrett, Robert Marks, Renata Teppo

"Mr. Rayburn . . . negotiated difficult passages with ease and finesse."
—South Bend Tribune

"James Rayburn has an energetic . . . unique style [that] dazzled the audience!"
—New York Post

- Always try to fit your resume on one page. If you are having trouble with this, you may be trying to say too much. Edit out any repetitive or unnecessary information, and shorten descriptions of earlier jobs where possible. Ask a friend you trust for feedback on what seems unnecessary or unimportant. For example, you may have included too many optional sections. Today, with the prevalence of the personal computer as a tool, there is no excuse for a poorly laid out resume. Experiment with variations until you are pleased with the result.

Remember that a resume is not an autobiography. Too much information will only get in the way. The more compact your resume, the easier it will be to review. If a person who is swamped with resumes looks at yours, catches the main points, and then calls you for an interview to fill in some of the details, your resume has already accomplished its task. A clear and concise resume makes for a happy reader and a good impression.

There are times when, despite extensive editing, the resume simply cannot fit on one page. In this case, the resume should be laid out on two pages in such a way that neither clarity nor appearance is compromised. Each page of a two-page resume should be marked clearly: the first should indicate "Page 1 of 2," and the second should include your name and the page number, for example, "Julia Ramirez—Page 2 of 2." The pages should then be stapled together. You may use a smaller font (in the same font as the body of your resume) for the page numbers. Place them at the bottom of page one and the top of page two. Again, spend the time now to experiment with the layout until you find one that looks good to you.

Always show your final layout to other people and ask them what they like or dislike about it, and what impresses them most when they read your resume. Make sure that their responses are the same as what you want to elicit from your prospective employer. If they aren't the same, you should continue to make changes until the necessary information is emphasized.

Proofreading

After you have finished typing the master copy of your resume and before you have it copied or printed, thoroughly check it for typing and spelling errors. Do not place all your trust in your computer's spellcheck function. Use an old editing trick and read the whole resume backward—start at the end and read it right to left and bottom to top. This can help you see the small errors or inconsistencies that are easy to overlook. Take time to do it right because a single error on a document this important can cause the reader to judge your attention to detail in a harsh light.

Have several people look at the finished resume just in case you've missed an error. Don't try to take a shortcut; not having an unbiased set of eyes examine your resume now could mean embarrassment later. Even experienced editors can easily overlook their own errors. Be thorough and conscientious with your proofreading so your first impression is a perfect one.

We have included the following rules of capitalization and punctuation to assist you in the final stage of creating your resume. Remember that resumes often require use of a shorthand style of writing that may include sentences without periods and other stylistic choices that break the standard rules of grammar. Be consistent in each section and throughout the whole resume with your choices.

RULES OF CAPITALIZATION

- Capitalize proper nouns, such as names of schools, colleges, and universities; names of companies; and brand names of products.

- Capitalize major words in the names and titles of books, tests, and articles that appear in the body of your resume.

- Capitalize words in major section headings of your resume.

- Do not capitalize words just because they seem important.

- When in doubt, consult a style manual such as *Words into Type* (Prentice Hall) or *The Chicago Manual of Style* (The University of Chicago Press). Your local library can help you locate these and other reference books. Many computer programs also have grammar help sections.

RULES OF PUNCTUATION

- Use commas to separate words in a series.

- Use a semicolon to separate series of words that already include commas within the series. (For an example, see the first rule of capitalization.)

- Use a semicolon to separate independent clauses that are not joined by a conjunction.

- Use a period to end a sentence.

- Use a colon to show that examples or details follow that will expand or amplify the preceding phrase.

- Avoid the use of dashes.

- Avoid the use of brackets.

- If you use any punctuation in an unusual way in your resume, be consistent in its use.

- Whenever you are uncertain, consult a style manual.

Putting Your Resume in Print

You will need to buy high-quality paper for your printer before you print your finished resume. Regular office paper is not good enough for resumes; the reviewer will probably think it looks flimsy and cheap. Go to an office supply store or copy shop and select a high-quality bond paper that will make a good first impression. Select colors like white, off-white, or possibly a light gray. In some industries, a pastel may be acceptable, but be sure the color and feel of the paper makes a subtle, positive statement about you. Nothing in the choice of paper should be loud or unprofessional.

If your computer printer does not reproduce your resume properly and produces smudged or stuttered type, either ask to borrow a friend's or take your disk (or a clean original) to a printer or copy shop for high-quality copying. If you anticipate needing a large number of copies, taking your resume to a copy shop or a printer is probably the best choice.

Hold a sheet of your unprinted bond paper up to the light. If it has a watermark, you will want to point this out to the person helping you with copies; the printing should be done so that the reader can read the print and see the watermark the right way up. Check each copy for smudges or streaks. This is the time to be a perfectionist—the results of your careful preparation will be well worth it.

Chapter 4

The Cover Letter

Once your resume has been assembled, laid out, and printed to your satisfaction, the next and final step before distribution is to write your cover letter. Though there may be instances where you deliver your resume in person, you will usually send it through the mail or online. Resumes sent through the mail always need an accompanying letter that briefly introduces you and your resume. The purpose of the cover letter is to get a potential employer to read your resume, just as the purpose of the resume is to get that same potential employer to call you for an interview.

Like your resume, your cover letter should be clean, neat, and direct. A cover letter usually includes the following information:

1. Your name and address (unless it already appears on your personal letterhead) and your phone number(s); see item 7.

2. The date.

3. The name and address of the person and company to whom you are sending your resume.

4. The salutation ("Dear Mr." or "Dear Ms." followed by the person's last name, or "To Whom It May Concern" if you are answering a blind ad).

5. An opening paragraph explaining why you are writing (for example, in response to an ad, as a follow-up to a previous meeting, at the suggestion of someone you both know) and indicating that you are interested in whatever job is being offered.

6. One or more paragraphs that tell why you want to work for the company and what qualifications and experiences you can bring to the position. This is a good place to mention some detail about

that particular company that makes you want to work for them; this shows that you have done some research before applying.

7. A final paragraph that closes the letter and invites the reviewer to contact you for an interview. This can be a good place to tell the potential employer which method would be best to use when contacting you. Be sure to give the correct phone number and a good time to reach you, if that is important. You may mention here that your references are available upon request.

8. The closing ("Sincerely" or "Yours truly") followed by your signature in a dark ink, with your name typed under it.

Your cover letter should include all of this information and be no longer than one page in length. The language used should be polite, businesslike, and to the point. Don't attempt to tell your life story in the cover letter; a long and cluttered letter will serve only to annoy the reader. Remember that you need to mention only a few of your accomplishments and skills in the cover letter. The rest of your information is available in your resume. If your cover letter is a success, your resume will be read and all pertinent information reviewed by your prospective employer.

Producing the Cover Letter

Cover letters should always be individualized because they are always written to specific individuals and companies. Never use a form letter for your cover letter or copy it as you would a resume. Each cover letter should be unique, and as personal and lively as possible. (Of course, once you have written and rewritten your first cover letter until you are satisfied with it, you can certainly use similar wording in subsequent letters. You may want to save a template on your computer for future reference.) Keep a hard copy of each cover letter so you know exactly what you wrote in each one.

There are sample cover letters in Chapter 6. Use them as models or for ideas of how to assemble and lay out your own cover letters. Remember that every letter is unique and depends on the particular circumstances of the individual writing it and the job for which he or she is applying.

After you have written your cover letter, proofread it as thoroughly as you did your resume. Again, spelling or punctuation errors are a sure sign of carelessness, and you don't want that to be a part of your first impression on a prospective employer. This is no time to trust your spellcheck function. Even after going through a spelling and grammar check, your cover letter should be carefully proofread by at least one other person.

Print the cover letter on the same quality bond paper you used for your resume. Remember to sign it, using a good dark-ink pen. Handle the letter and resume carefully to avoid smudging or wrinkling, and mail them together in an appropriately sized envelope. Many stores sell matching envelopes to coordinate with your choice of bond paper.

Keep an accurate record of all resumes you send out and the results of each mailing. This record can be kept on your computer, in a calendar or notebook, or on file cards. Knowing when a resume is likely to have been received will keep you on track as you make follow-up phone calls.

About a week after mailing resumes and cover letters to potential employers, contact them by telephone. Confirm that your resume arrived and ask whether an interview might be possible. Be sure to record the name of the person you spoke to and any other information you gleaned from the conversation. It is wise to treat the person answering the phone with a great deal of respect; sometimes the assistant or receptionist has the ear of the person doing the hiring.

You should make a great impression with the strong, straightforward resume and personalized cover letter you have just created. We wish you every success in securing the career of your dreams!

Sample Resumes

This chapter contains dozens of sample resumes for people pursuing a wide variety of jobs and careers.

There are many different styles of resumes in terms of graphic layout and presentation of information. These samples represent people with varying amounts of education and experience. Use them as models for your own resume. Choose one resume or borrow elements from several different resumes to help you design your own.

PEDRO VALEZ

232 Forest Avenue
Miami, Florida 33513
(305) 555-5644

Performance Experience

Orchestral Experience
Florida State University Orchestra
Florida State Band
American World Orchestra

Chamber Music Experience
FSU Contemporary Players (Bass Clarinet)
University Jazz Quartet
Willson Quintet

Recitals
Coral Beach Holiday Inn "Holiday Showcase":
    December 2001–2003
Florida-for-the-Arts Young Artist Series: April 2002

Other Experience
Boardwalk Club Piano Bar: weekly gig featuring the
    Willson Quintet, 2003–Present
Interlochen Arts Academy: Summer 1997

Training/Teachers

Clarinet (B flat and Bass)
Stephen Canby
Geraldine Hicks
Alto Saxophone
Josh Lindberg
Jazz Theory
Josh Lindberg
Renee Gonzales

Master Classes and Coaches
Howard James
Bennie Girbaud
The Davis T. Henderson Quartet

Education

Florida State University at Coral Beach, 2003
B.A. Music Theory; Music Performance minor

Ginny Rae Bell
Comedienne

P.O. Box 2282   GinnyBell@xxx.com
San Jose, CA 95125   510-555-7382

STAND-UP

Zanies   Ariel's Big Comics (ABC)
House of Comedy   The Funny Farm
Bay City Backyard   Cut-up Club

COMMERCIALS

Little Romeo's West (Restaurant Hostess)   Prince Productions
California Lotto (Woman with Umbrella)   J. B. Hill Inc.

RADIO/TELEVISION

What's So Funny?
College Radio Show, WUCB-UC Berkeley
  • Classic Comedy Routines
  • Call-ins

Get a Life!
Local Cable Access Show, San Jose Cable Company
  • Stand-up
  • Human Disinterested Stories
  • View Mail
  • Joke-of-the-Week

SHOWCASE PRODUCTION

A Laugh Riot, House of Comedy, Berkeley, CA
  • Local and Greater West Coast talent
  • Standing room only

Self-produced comedy showcase. Two nights of stand-up and musical acts at well-known comedy club. Contract optioned for 2004–2005.

TRAINING

Elaine Fingerhut School for the Comically Insane (founding member)
Rob Morton Comedy Workshop

University of California at Berkeley
B.A. Political Science with a Television and Radio minor

Jennifer T. Modigliano

6342 Rock Creek Road
Stillwater, OK 74800
(405) 555-4323
J.Modigliano@xxx.com

Objective

To obtain a stage management position in a small theater company with possible performance opportunities.

Acting Experience

Felicity / *City of Angels* / University Theater (University of Oklahoma)
Helena / *All's Well That Ends Well* / University Theater
Gina / *The Wild Duck* / University Student Theater

Stage Manager Experience

Stage
As You Like It
Spell #7
Three Sisters

Musical
Sweeney Todd / University Theater
Company / University Student Theater
You're a Good Man, Charlie Brown / University Student Theater
The Mikado / University Student Theater

Additional Experience

Assistant Stage Manager / University Theater / two years
Set Designers Workshop / three years
Costume Shop / two years

Modern Dance classes / five semesters
The Tonsiltones / female a capella group / three years
The Laugh Machine / comedy improvisation / one year

Education

University of Oklahoma at Tulsa / B.A. degree expected December 2004

Caren Wilson   *Vocalist*

222 Central Avenue
Baton Rouge, LA 70822
504-555-4788

Clubs

Capetown Mines
Cajun Caties
Jazz Etcetera
Forrest Hicks/Home of the Blues
Casa de Jazz
Figure Eight Club
Catfish Club

Showcase

"Cleopatra's Girls"
"Get Up and Sing"
"One Night in Tunisia"

Shows

Jelly's Last Jam	Tea Rose Theatre
Ain't Misbehavin'	Tea Rose Theatre
Po'	Cherie Playhouse
For Your Eyes Only	Tea Rose Theatre
Church-Mouse Charlie	Cherie Playhouse

Choirs

Louisiana Gospel Choir (2000 Grammy winners)
Wilson Trio (family gospel trio)
Mt. Vernon Baptist Church Choir

Len Masada, Guitar

124 W. Burnside
Hazlet, NJ 07730
Home: (908) 555-2454
Cellular: (908) 555-2455

Performance Experience/Classical

Bella Aura Trio
- Classical guitar trio, founded 1997.
- Trio has performed throughout New York metropolitan area, tristate region, and suburbs.
- Originally conceived as part of University Theatre Arts Program, New York University.

Solo Performances
- Recital at Third Presbyterian, Orange, NJ.
- Recital for National Renaissance Week, Hoboken, NJ.
- King John's Faire (Renaissance Fair), Pallisades, NJ.

Popular Experience

Mike Mike
- Five-member funk and dance band, electric guitar.
- Weekly gig at House of Funk.
- Shows throughout New York and New Jersey.

Recordings

With Bella Aura Trio
- *Bella Aura Trio* (debut album)   Reno Records
- *Bella Aura Trio: Sweete Love*   EMI Records, Inc.
- *Bella Aura: New Beginnings*   Sony Classical

With Mike Mike
- *I'm Not Crazy (Yet)*   MCA Records, Inc.

ALTHEA MORRIS
• • •
433 8TH STREET • ATLANTA, GA 30312
(404) 555-4655 (SERVICE) • ALTHEA.MORRIS@XXX.COM

• • • COMMERCIALS/JINGLES

Atlanta Bell	Fantastic Travel
Atlanta Cable	MARTIX
Century 21	Georgia Peaches
Harlan Ford	Canape Waterbeds
Jewel Food Stores	Tidy Diaper Service
MacGruders Groceries	Atlanta Gazette
Mattress Etcetera	East Point Cadillac

• • • INDUSTRIALS/VOICE-OVERS

Popeye's, In-house
Metropolitan Cable Company, In-house
Wilson Pools Ltd., Cooper-Wells Inc.

• • • MUSICAL THEATRE

Ensemble member of the Southern and Southwestern touring
companies of *Showboat*, 2001–2003

• • • EDUCATION/TRAINING

B.A. in American and European History
Spelman College

• • • AGENT

Lana Harris Artists Inc.
55 Continental Drive
Atlanta, Georgia 30301
(404) 555-4100
L.Harris@xxx.com

Carol Lee

1816 Birch Street
Chevy Chase, MD 20045
301-555-4688
Carol.Lee@xxx.com

Objective

A full-time position as a vocal accompanist at a well-respected music conservatory.

Education

B.M. Vocal Accompaniment Program
Peabody Conservatory of Music, 2000

Experience

Private studio lessons

- Accompanied three vocal studios with a minimum of fifteen students each at the undergraduate and graduate levels.
- Shared responsibilities as accompanist with two fellow pianists and accompanist majors.
- Accompanied fifteen to twenty half-hour lessons per week.
- Held coaching sessions for a total of thirty hours per week.

Recitals

- Played approximately twenty-five recitals per year as part of the accompanist program (unpaid).
- Offered additional coaching in preparation for recitals.

Opera

- Coached ten graduate voice majors as part of the opera studio program.
- Substituted for faculty accompanists during absence.
- Assisted the director in scene preparation.

References

Available upon request.

Joshua Frank
Countertenor

122 S. Chaswell
Hoboken, NJ 07030
(201) 555-4595
J.Frank@xxx.com

CONCERT APPEARANCES

Messiah, Handel	Marks Hall, NYC
Gloria, Vivaldi	New Jersey Choral Society
Cantata No. 140, Mozart	Millard College of Music
Messiah, Handel	Millard College of Music
Israel in Egypt, Handel	Millard College of Music

RECITALS

Hermit Songs, Barber	Hoboken Arts League
Let Us Garlands Bring, Finzi	Millard College of Music
Exultate, Jubilate, Mozart	Hoboken Arts League
Ah, Lo Previdi! K. 272, Mozart	Millard College of Music

OPERATIC ROLES

Acis, *Acis and Galatea*	Trenton Lyric Opera
Aeneas, *Dido and Aeneas*	New Jersey Opera
Florio, *Ascanio in Alba*	Millard College of Music

AWARDS

The Frederick E. Stern Award for Historical Performance Studies
Millard Performance Scholarship

FUTURE ENGAGEMENTS

Achsas, *Joshua*	New Jersey Opera
Requiem, Mozart	New Jersey Choral Society

TRAINING

Voice:	Jonathan Rudman, Carol Jonas
Historical Performance:	Eileen Hillman, Thomas McCall, Alan Meeks

Master of Music in Voice Performance, Millard College of Music, NJ
Bachelor of Music in General Music, Piano Concentration, Millard College

DANICA HARRIS

Coloratura Soprano
508 9th Street • Brooklyn, NY 11215 • (718) 555-3735

HEIGHT: 5'2" • HAIR/EYES: BROWN • WEIGHT: 120 • BIRTH DATE: 6/1/76

ROLES PERFORMED

The Magic Flute, Queen of the Night, Brooklyn Opera	2004
The Italian Girl in Algiers, Elvira, Brooklyn Opera	2003
Tales of Hoffman, Olympia, Madison Opera	2002
Street Scene, Mrs. Fiorentino, Madison Opera	2002
Sister Angelica, First Novice, Madison Opera	2001
The Pirates of Penzance, Mabel, Madison Theater	2000
West Side Story, Maria, Blue Lake (WI)	1998
The Apple Grove, Girl, Blue Lake	1998

CONCERT AND ORATORIO

Faure Requiem, soloist, Trenton, NJ	2002
Carmina Burana, soloist, Madison, WI	2002
Bach St. John Passion, soloist, Madison, WI	2001
Messiah, soloist, Milwaukee, WI	2000

TRAINING

Teachers: Edward Eslton, Marcia Crawford, Elsie Pitts
Coaches: John Bergeron, Roger Thomas, Kelly O'Rourke
Instruments: piano, organ, flute
Dance: ballet, jazz, tap

EDUCATION

Madison Conservatory of Music
Madison, Wisconsin
B.M. Vocal Performance, 2002

MARIA GONZALEZ
Double Bass

Home Address
2565 Cooper Avenue
San Francisco, CA 93120
613-555-4788

School Address
114 East 23rd Street #16B
New York, NY 10018
212-555-0213

EDUCATION AND TRAINING

Juilliard School of Music
Bachelor of Music: Double Bass Performance with Vaughan Chambers
Secondary Cello Studies with Denise Novello
Date of Graduation: May 2002

Private study with Robert Pytorski: San Francisco, California
Principal Double Bassist, San Francisco Symphony
Dates of study: September 1994–July 1998, Summer 1995

PROFESSIONAL ORCHESTRAL EXPERIENCE

Greenwich, NY Symphony Orchestra: principal	2000–present
San Francisco Symphony Orchestra	2001
Mt. Vernon, NY Chamber Players	1998–2000

OTHER ORCHESTRAL EXPERIENCE

Juilliard Chamber Orchestra: principal	2001–present
Juilliard Contemporary Ensemble: assistant principal	1999–present
Juilliard Orchestra: assistant principal	1998–present
San Francisco All-City Orchestra	1997–1998

REFERENCES

References are available on request.

DONNY BEALE
ACTOR
SAG/AFTRA
20 W. Adams Ave.
Hoboken, NJ 07021
(607) 555-6024

Height: 5'7"
Weight: 135
Hair: Dark Brown
Eyes: Blue

THEATRE

Carrie's Nightmare, Jon, Grove Theater
Travesties, Ernest, New English Theater
Wishful Thinking, Sam/Host, Grove Theater
Walter's Secret Life, Walter Mitty, Theatre on Hudson
The Ann Davis Story, Hotel Patron, Spin City Playhouse

FILM

Dixie Lilly, Bartender, Fox Entertainment
W. C. Fields Lives, Concierge, Turner Television
Jewel of the Nile, Cab Driver, Paramount Studios

COMMERCIALS

New York State Lotto, Don Harper Productions
Video King, Colgate, Inc.
Matrix Paper Co., in-house
Higgins Chevrolet, Family Productions Co.

MUSICALS

The King and I, King of Siam, Tawny Lane Theater
Les Misérables, Marius, Tawny Lane Theater
The Sound of Music, Rolf, Sloane Playhouse

TRAINING

Acting: Jonathan Stull, Fred Zimmer
Movement: Elaine Iwa

SPECIAL SKILLS

Various dialects/accents, lighting and tech, gymnastics, juggling, softball

THOMAS FAYE
43 Sanger Avenue
Boulder, CO 39828
(303) 555-0829
Tom.Faye@xxx.com

OBJECTIVE: To obtain a summer position as a drama counselor at a performing arts camp.

EXPERIENCE: **Assistant Director**
Rockwell High School - Boulder, Colorado
- Assisted the director of an award-winning high school theater program.
- Duties included supervising attendance, rehearsal schedules, and prop management.
- Supervised lighting and stage crew.
- Directed students in individual scenes as a part of advanced acting class curriculum.

Counselor/Dramatics Specialist
Jewish Community Center Day Camps - Rock Creek, Colorado
- Organized theater games and weekly talent shows for children ages 6 to 13.
- Daily counselor duties.

EDUCATION: Rockwell High School - Boulder, Colorado
GPA: 3.6
Expected graduation date, June 2005.

SPECIAL SKILLS: Acrobatics, ice skating, skiing, hockey, comedy improvisation, photography, and sculpture.

REFERENCES: Manny Zitnik, Director of Theater Arts, Rockwell High School, (303) 555-6674.

More available upon request.

Dianna Kurako
Conductor

533 Sharon Avenue, Apt. #3
Memphis, TN 37402
Home: (615) 555-7441
Cellular: (615) 555-0091

Operetta/Musical Theater

The Most Happy Fella	Memphis Crown Theater
The Student Prince	Memphis Crown Theater
Die Fledermaus (The Bat)	Memphis Crown Theater
The Mikado	Memphis Savoyards
The Pirates of Penzance	Memphis Savoyards
Patience	Memphis Savoyards
The Yeomen of the Guard	Memphis Savoyards
Trial by Jury	Memphis Savoyards
The Gondoliers	University of Tennessee
Ruddigore	University of Tennessee

Orchestral

Adagio/Barber	Orchestra Memphis
Rodeo/Copeland	Orchestra Memphis
Mass/Bernstein (excerpts)	Bernstein Fest/Nashville
L'Histoire du Soldat/Stravinsky	University of Tennessee

Education

Conducting Teacher and Coaches: Larry Beck, Janice Howe, Franco Beretta, Lisle Carter

University of Tennessee, Chattanooga, TN
B.A. Sociology major, Music minor

Carter Henderson, *Trombone*

5767 Edgemore Drive
St. Louis, MO 63115
(314) 555-2230
C.Henderson@xxx.com

Professional Experience

St. Louis Symphony Orchestra	2001–present
Brass St. Louis (founder)	1999–present
Opera Theatre of St. Louis	1998–2002
Missouri Civic Symphony	1996–1998

Other Experience

St. Louis Conservatory Opera Orchestra
St. Louis Conservatory Orchestra
St. Louis Conservatory Baroque Ensemble
St. Louis Conservatory Trombone Choir
Aspen Festival Orchestra

Festivals

Ravinia Festival/Stern Institute for Brass and Winds	Highland Park, IL
Aspen Music Festival	Aspen, CO

Education

Bachelor of Music: Trombone Performance
St. Louis Conservatory, 1996
Principal Teacher: Patrick Hand

Major Conductors: Sir Alan Welkes, Samuel Cohn, Desie Hillis-Patel, Colin MacKinney, Donald Kimbrough, Majorie Lewin

TRINA WEISSMAN

4918 S. Millard   Agent: Don Weissman
Lake Persephone, NY 10137   (212) 555-0200
(212) 555-0270

Hair: Auburn   Height: 4'10"
Eyes: Brown   Age: 14

STAGE AND MUSICAL THEATER

Joseph and the Amazing Technicolor Dreamcoat, Chorus, Shubert Theater
Annie, Annie, Theatre on the Lake
You're a Good Man, Charlie Brown, Lucy, Theatre on the Lake
The Sound of Music, Gretl, Theatre on the Lake
Snow White in the Black Forest, Primrose, Starr Children's Theatre
Alice in Wonderland, Mad Hatter, Starr Children's Theatre
Give My Regards to Broadway, Ms. Hollywood, Starr Children's Theatre
The King and I, Ensemble, Starr Children's Theatre

COMMERCIALS

Pampers, Searle/Ralston
McDonald's, Ryan McCall Inc.
Barbie Playhouse, Mattel in-house
Captain Crunch (voice-over), Frasier Productions, Ltd.

TRAINING

Acting: Lana Wood, Danny Zucker–Starr Children's Theatre
Singing: Leslie Goodwin (private), Joyful Noise Children's Chorus (7 years)
Dance: Ballet, Tap (4 years), Modern (2 years)–Metropolitan School of Dance

SPECIAL SKILLS AND INTERESTS

Songwriting, Creative Writing, Swimming, Diving,
Gymnastics, Ice Skating, Drawing

SARAH J. LINDENBAUM

HOME ADDRESS	SCHOOL ADDRESS
152 North Avenue	33 Maple Avenue
Wilmette, IL 60122	Ann Arbor, MI 49023
(847) 555-3388	(413) 555-6672

OBJECTIVE
Cello teaching and performing

EDUCATION
University of Michigan School of Music, 1989.
Ann Arbor, Michigan.
- Music Education major, Cello Performance minor.
- Cumulative GPA 3.53.
- Cello studies with Lottie Liebman and Jonathan Carter.

TEACHING EXPERIENCE
- Taught cello in the Ann Arbor Public School System, 1997–2002.
- Lecturer and part-time cello instructor, University of Michigan School of Music, 2002–present.
- Teaching emphasis on historical performance, Renaissance period, and chamber music.

LARGE ENSEMBLES
- University of Michigan Orchestra, Section Principal for guest conductors Jeremy Dial and Sir George Bishop, 1984–1989.
- University Cello Octet, 1986–1988.
- East Lansing Civic Orchestra, Assistant Principal, 1989–1994, Principal 1994–1997.
- Wilmette Chamber Orchestra, Section Principal, Summers, 1992–present.

SMALL ENSEMBLES
- Extensive experience in romantic, modern, and contemporary periods as well as baroque historical performance.
- Coaches include members of the Nouveau String Quartet and distinguished faculty of the Central Midwest Music Camp and Lake Forest College in addition to University training.
- Coprincipal University Chamber Ensemble, 1987–1989.

Beverly Whitfield

61 Sanders Avenue, #302
New Haven, CT 07450
(203) 555-1644
B.Whitfield@xxx.com

Height: 5'3"
Weight: 120
Hair: Dark Brown
Eyes: Hazel
Birth Date: 5/4/84

Stage Experience

Hamlet, Ophelia, Yale University Theater
Wine in the Wilderness, Tommy, Yale Little Theater
Joe Turner's Come and Gone, Molly, Yale University Theater
The Caucasian Chalk Circle, Peasant, Yale University Theater
Love's Labor's Lost, Princess, Yale University Theater
The Children's Hour, Mary, Yale Little Theater

Scene Work

The Women, Mary, Yale University Drama
The Taming of the Shrew, Kate, Yale University Drama
A Midsummer Night's Dream, Hermia, Yale University Drama
The Importance of Being Ernest, Cecily, Yale University Drama

Related Experience

Assistant Stage Manager, Yale University Drama (2 years)
Set Designer, Yale University Drama (1 year)
Costume/Makeup Assistant, Yale University Theater (3 years)

Education

Yale University
B.A. in English with an emphasis on Theater
Degree expected, 2005

Acting teachers: Connie Jenkins, Lana Haggen, Jim Beale, Gerald Fuller

Dance experience: ballet, jazz (2 years), folk dance (8 years)

PENELOPE RENATO
Mezzo-Soprano

970 W. Armitage • Chicago, IL 60614 • (312) 555-2875

Hair: Light Brown
Eyes: Blue
Height: 5'6" Weight: 140

Roles Performed
La Traviata, Flora, Chicago Opera Theater
Cosi fan Tutte, Dorabella (cover), DePaul University
La Cenerentola, Title role, DePaul University
Le Nozze di Figaro, Cherubino, DePaul University
Werther, Charlotte, Chautauqua Opera
Hansel and Gretel, Hansel, DePaul University
The Yeomen of the Guard, Phoebe, Northwestern University

Oratorio/Concert Performances
Handel, *Israel in Egypt*, Wheaton Symphony
Mahler, *Symphony IV*, DePaul University
Bach, *Magnificat*, DePaul University
Handel, *Messiah*, Northwestern University

Voice Teachers - Raquel Gordon (present), Nicholai Moss, Lena Armstrong
Conductors - George Hill, Fiona Rossi, John Bender, James Washington Banks
Coaches - Elaine Kirsch, Edward Grant, Hugh Stein, Richard Liotta

Awards and Honors
First Place Winner, Loggia Competition, Orzo, Italy
John F. Stein Award for Musical Excellence, DePaul University
Fellowship recipient, Northwestern University Young Artist Program

Education
Master of Music, DePaul University School of Music, Chicago, IL
Bachelor of Music, DePaul University School of Music, Chicago, IL

ELIA M. GREY
Comedian/Actor
AFTRA

Capri Artists Ltd.
130 W. 10th St., Suite 302
New York, NY 10012
(212) 555-5434

CLUB APPEARANCES

Don't Tell Mama	The Cellar
Harpo's	First Up Comedy Club
The Duplex	Joujou
Rose's Place	The Improv Late Nite
Waki's	Emcee/Metro Cruises

FILM
The Jury, Club Dancer, Universal
Business as Usual, Club Patron, Touchstone
Baby Talk, Woman in Park, Warner Brothers

TELEVISION SERIES
"One Life to Live," Student, ABC
"The City," Bar Patron, ABC
"The Minister's Wife," Mourner, WNET-Great Performances

TELEVISION/RADIO
"Arts Watch," Host/Writer/Production, KSNO-Radio, Aspen, CO
"Human Interest Weekly," Reporter, KSKI-TV, Aspen, CO

THEATRE
Long Ago and Far Away, Jantzi, Langston Hughes Theatre
Passage of Time, Helen, Printer Play Theatre
Solomon's Song, Sheba, National Black Theatre
South Pacific, Blood Mary, Aspen Theatre

TRAINING
COMEDY:	Dan Stein Comedy Workshop
	Ellen Goodwin Comedy Binge Workshop
ACTING:	Joel Cohen Theatre Workshop, NY
	National Black Theatre Institute, NY
VOICE/MUSIC:	Aspen Music Festival: Janet Winters, Lynn Troy

B.A. Columbia University   Sociology/Romance Languages

SKILLS
Fluent in Spanish and French
Dialects: English, Cockney, French, Italian, Australian, Russian, New York, New York Jewish, cartoon/kids' voices

MARCUS ANTHONY ALTMONT
MODEL
152 Alanis Road
Minton, Connecticut 06457
830/555-2587
www.MarcusAltmont.com

Height: 6'2"
Weight: 190
Hair: Black
Eyes: Brown

PROFESSIONAL EXPERIENCE

PRINT
J. Crew
Lands' End
Tommy Hilfiger
Abercrombie & Fitch
Saks Fifth Avenue
Clinique for Men
Ralph Lauren Home

TELEVISION
Calvin Klein Fragrances
Bally's Total Fitness
New York Public Library
Bilford's Bistro and Brewery
Big Brothers (New York)
YMCA (New York)
Audio Consultants
Connecticut Public Television

FILM
When Harry Met Sally (extra)

EDUCATION AND TRAINING
B.A., Performing Arts, University of Connecticut (Storrs)
Modeling: TalentExpress

References Available on Request

------- MICHAEL DODGE -------
------ 18 CRESTWELL LANE ------
---- DUBUQUE, IA 52008 ----
---- 312-555-0980 ----

OBJECTIVE

Position in arts management firm, utilizing skills in organization and performance experience in the field of music.

EDUCATION

Grinnell College, Grinnell, Iowa
B.A. Music, Performance Emphasis (Harp)
Graduated, May 2004
Principal Teacher: Elaine DeNoone

ACCOMPLISHMENTS

Performed as solo, chamber, and orchestra harpist.

Competed in regional and scholastic competitions.

America's #1 College Orchestra, Disneyland, CA.
• Played 10 to 15 performances weekly.
• Attended weekly clinics with various managers and artists.

Peer Counselor, Student Support and Placement Services, Grinnell College.

Tutor, Student/Youth Assistance Program, Grinnell, IA.

EMPLOYMENT HISTORY

Harvey Hall, Grinnell College - Head Usher
(2 years)
• Supervised six ushers for campus performances.
• Prepared ushering schedule.
• Ushered for performances.

Grinnell Admissions Office - Assistant (2 years)
• Basic receptionist duties: phones, filing, collating, typing.
• Assisted and fielded calls for admissions director and staff that varied between 7 and 12 people.

Iowa Symphony Orchestra - Publicity Intern
• Summer intern for midsize symphony orchestra.
• Assembled press scrapbook, assisted with mass mailings in conjunction with ticket office.

INTERESTS

Skiing, swimming, biking, working with children, psychology, art history.

Sabrina Mills

85 Walnut Street • Fairhaven, MA 02744 • 508/555-9845

Height: 5'5"
Voice: Alto/Belt
Weight: 125
Hair: Black
Eyes: Green
Equity Eligible

Stage Experience

National Tours

Joseph and the Amazing Technicolor Dreamcoat, Narrator, Winner, 2004 Fox Award
Jesus Christ Superstar, Mary Magdalene, Revival
Fame! The Musical, Doris, Canadian/U.S. Tour

Professional (Local)

The Pirates of Penzance, Ruth, Auditorium Theatre
A Little Night Music, Petra, Emerson Theatre
The Wiz (Revival), Miss One, Apollo Theatre

Miscellaneous

Les Misérables, Eponine, Medford Theater Group
Pippin, Fastrada, Boston U. Players
Cats, Rumpleteaser, Boston College Theater
West Side Story, Teresa, Boston College Theater

Training

Voice (Classical): Mirella Amato
Belt: Fran Lieber, Jon Errol
Dance: Liza Jenkins Studio, Boston

Education

B.F.A. Boston College, 2002

References

Available upon request

•Aaron Thomas•

bass-baritone

27 Spring Street • Yellow Springs, OH 44052
A.Thomas@xxx.com
(216) 555-8763

•Opera and Musical Theater

The Old Maid and the Thief	Bob	Cleveland Music College
La Boheme	Colline	Cleveland Music College
Le Nozze di Figaro	Antonio	Cleveland Music College
	Figaro (cover)	
The Mikado	Mikado	College Savoyards
Pippin	Charlemagne	Star Dinner Theater
South Pacific	Emile de Becque	Star Dinner Theater
My Fair Lady	Col. Pickering	Star Dinner Theater

•Oratorio

Creation	Haydn	Cleveland College Chorus
Messiah	Handel	Cleveland College Chorus
Magnificat	Bach	Cleveland College Chorus
Judas Maccabeus	Handel	Cleveland College Chorus

•Education

Cleveland Music College, Bachelor's degree, Voice, 2001
Summer Abroad Program: Piazza, Italy, 1999
Teachers: Jane Leeds, Karl Henderson, Cynthia Harding
Dance: Tap (2 years), Jazz (3 years), Modern (1 year)

Derrick Johnson, Bass

245 N. Abbott Dr.
Bloomington, IN 46802
812-555-6144

Roles Performed

Nick Shadow	*The Rake's Progress*	IU Opera
Commendatore	*Don Giovanni*	IU Opera
Crespel	*The Tales of Hoffman*	IU Opera
Dulcamara	*The Elixer of Love*	IU Opera

Roles Studied

Faust	*Faust*	IU Opera Studio
Sarastro	*The Magic Flute*	IU Opera Studio
Horace Tabor	*The Ballad of Baby Doe*	IU Opera Studio

Theater

Jim	*The Glass Menagerie*	Fair Lake Academy
Zach	*Untamed Heart*	Fair Lake Academy
Crow	*Mr. Monday*	Fair Lake Academy

Education

B.M. Vocal Performance, Indiana University, degree expected 2005

Honors Student, Fair Lake Academy, Fair Lake, Indiana
Areas of Concentration: Theater and Music

Skills

Acting, Dance, Juggling, Stage Combat

Instruments

Piano, Acoustic Guitar, Saxophone

YUKI MIZURA

BASSOON

PRESENT ADDRESS
145 Main Street, #2
Evanston, IL 60602
(847) 555-8103

HOME ADDRESS
25 Seponsette Road
Pleasant, NJ 10540
(201) 555-4282

ORCHESTRAL EXPERIENCE

Northwestern University Chamber Players–two years
Northwestern University Orchestra–three years
Chicago Civic Orchestra–principal, two years
All-State Orchestra–principal, four years
Juilliard Pre-College Orchestra–principal, two years
Tristate Youth Orchestra–three years

ENSEMBLE EXPERIENCE

Northwestern University Wind Ensemble–principal, one year
University Chamber Winds–three years

SPECIAL HONORS

Northwestern Concerto Competition, Third Place, 2003
New York Tristate Wind Ensemble, principal, 2001
Leonard Bernstein Festival New England, participant, 1999

PRIVATE TEACHERS

Kevin Sheehan, current teacher
Manfred Geller, principal, Chicago Symphony
Jonathan Woods, retired principal, New York Philharmonic

EDUCATION

Northwestern University, B. Mus. Bassoon Performance
Degree expected in May 2004

Juilliard Pre-College division, 1995–1999

Martha Oki, Oboe

68447 Oahu Drive
Honolulu, Hawaii 96732
808-555-4700
M.Oki@xxx.com

Education
B. Mus. (Performance) Cincinnati Institute of Music, 1995

Performing Experience
Associate Principal Oboe, Honolulu Symphony
Principal Oboe, Dayton Philharmonic
Principal Oboe, Ohio Civic Orchestra
Assistant Principal Oboe, Scranton Symphony

Teaching Experience
Associate Professor, Dayton University
Guest Lecturer, College of Wooster, University of Honolulu

Honors
Runner-up Principal Oboe, Cincinnati Orchestra
Finalist Principal Oboe, Philadelphia Symphony

Summer Festivals
Principal Oboe, Spoleto Festival
Fellow, Aspen Music Festival
Fellow, Wildwood Music Festival

Teachers and Conductors
Robert Klein, Principal Oboe, Cincinnati Orchestra
Joseph Cade, Professor of Oboe, Cincinnati Institute of Music
Sarah Bedell, Conductor, Ohio Civic Orchestra
Joachim Andres, Director, Honolulu Youth Symphony

Linda Whitman
Violin

Present Address
250 Massachusetts Ave. #2
Boston, MA 02115
(617) 555-2204

Home Address
16 Timber Lane
North Ridge, RI 02904
(303) 555-8785

Education

New England Conservatory
B.M. degree expected: 2005
Joachim Meyer, Principal Teacher

Orchestral Engagements

New England Conservatory Orchestra (coprincipal 2nd violin)
Providence Youth Orchestra
Rhode Island All-State Orchestra (concertmaster)
North Ridge High School Orchestra (concertmaster)

Chamber Music Ensembles/Festivals

"Sommerville" String Quartet
Tanglewood Music Festival
New England Youth Chamber Arts Program

Awards

Lisbon Young Artist Competition, New England Region, Finalist
Concerto Winner, North Ridge High School
North Ridge Scholarship for Arts and Music, Winner

SANDRA MURDOCH, *violinist*

3807 N. California
Chicago, IL 60618
(312) 555-3837
S.Murdoch@xxx.com

EDUCATION

New England Conservatory of Music
Boston, MA
- Master's degree in Violin Performance, 2000
- Bachelor's degree in Violin Performance, 1997

St. Louis Conservatory of Music
St. Louis, MO
1995–1997

TRAINING

Principal Teachers: Jonathan Baeher, Gabriel Talon, Jorge Ribas

Coaches: David Lerner, Parnell Gibson, Lottie Spelling, Colin Furth

PERFORMANCE EXPERIENCE

- Civic Orchestra of Chicago
- Illinois Symphony
- New England Conservatory Orchestra
- Sarasota Music Festival
- Hansen International Festival

TEACHING EXPERIENCE

- Merit Music Program (Chicago, IL)
- American Conservatory of Music (Chicago, IL)
- Sherwood Conservatory (Chicago, IL)
- New England Conservatory (Boston, MA)

Sean Burke
Tuba

134 N. College Park
Rochester, NY 11966
Sean.Burke@xxx.com
(212) 555-6025

Education

Bachelor of Music (Tuba Performance) - Eastman School of Music, 2004
Aspen Festival School - Aspen, Colorado, Summer 2001
Mills High School - Takoma Springs, Washington, 1999

Professional Experience

Tubist, The American Wind Ensemble, Rochester, NY, presently
Tubist, The New Jersey Chamber Orchestra
Tubist, The Lincoln Brass Quintet, Rochester, NY, Northeast Summer Tour

Other Orchestral Experience

Tubist, The Eastman Orchestra, 2000-2004
Tubist, The Eastman Mixed Choir Orchestra - West Coast Tour, spring 2003
Tubist, The Aspen Festival Orchestra, summer 2001
Tubist, Seattle Youth Symphony, 1996-1999

Teachers and Other References

Daniel Bowdoin, Principal Tubist, New York State Orchestra
Linwood Miller, Professor of Tuba, Eastman School of Music
Johann Behr, Conductor, Seattle Youth Symphony

Stanley Beltzman

Trumpet

22 Ridge Avenue • Lexington, MA 02113
S.Beltzman@xxx.com • (617) 555-3212

Orchestral Engagements

- New England Conservatory Orchestra–principal
- NEC Opera Orchestra–principal
- Hartt Symphony and Opera Orchestras–principal
- Tanglewood Festival Orchestra and Chamber Orchestra

Other Ensembles

- NEC Honors Brass Quintet
- NEC Wind Ensemble
- Hartt Jazz Ensemble
- Hartt Contemporary Players

Recital

- Jordan Hall First Night, Boston, MA (NEC)–benefit for renovation
- Second Presbyterian Church, Lexington, MA
- St. Augusta Church, Hartford, CT

Awards

- New England Conservatory Graduate Award
- Hartt School of Music Performance Scholarship
- Tanglewood Festival Performance Scholarship

Education

New England Conservatory of Music–M.M. 2002

Hartt School of Music–B.M. 2000
Teachers:
- Rudolph Blintz, Boston Symphony Orchestra
- Mason Friml–American Symphony
- Gabriel Thompson–Canadian Brass Quintet

barry kim   actor/singer

16 Brookfield Road • Hartford, CT 07450
(203) 555-7879 • B.Kim@xxx.com

Height: 5'7" • Weight: 135 • Hair and Eyes: Black

theater

Much Ado About Nothing	Claudio
Our Town	Tom
Tom Jones	Highwayman

musical theater

The King and I	The King
Amahl and the Night Visitors	Amahl
The Secret Garden	Colin
Pippin	Charlemagne

choral

Musical Excerpts:

Carousel*	*Little Shop of Horrors**
The Fantasticks*	*South Pacific*
A Little Night Music*	*The Wiz*

Solo Classical:

Chichester Psalms (Bernstein)
Requiem (Faure)
Requiem (Lloyd Webber)

*Soloist

Page 1 of 2

education

Ethel Barrymore High School for the Performing Arts
LaFayette, NY
Graduation Date: June 2, 2004

Curriculum includes:

Acting	Dance (Ballet, Tap)
Singing	Improvisation
Fencing/Stage Combat	Mime/Character

Hartt Performance Center for Young Artists
Hartford, CT
Summers, 1998 to present

additional training

Private Voice Lessons	2 years	Phillip Theopholis
Private Piano Lessons	5 years	Deanna Harris

related skills and hobbies

Debate, forensics, play writing, baseball, hiking, and fishing

references

Available upon request

Bernardo Alti, Composer

333 Central Park West, Apt. 5
New York, NY 10023
212-555-5876
B.Alti@xxx.com

✳ Education

Mannes College of Music
Master of Music, 2004

The Juilliard School
Master of Music, 2001
Bachelor of Music, 2000

The Juilliard School
Piano Studies, Pre-College Division
1994-1996

Marcia Umberto, Musical Academy
Piano and Clarinet Studies
1986-1994

✳ Principal Teachers

Walter Stanley
Marcia Umberto
Veronique Pujo
Jean-Luc Mouton
Hugh Waldman

✳ Teaching

The Juilliard School
Teaching Assistant in Music Theory
1999-2001

✶ *Awards*

Merit Scholarship, Mannes College of Music, 1997

Recipient, Leonard Bernstein Composition Award, 2000

✶ *Skills & Interests*

Fluent in Spanish and French
Piano
Oboe
Photography
Modern Dance

✶ *Partial List of Compositions*

"Divertimento" for Winds and Percussion
"Elias"–Quartet for Woodwinds and Timpani
"Fanfare" for Brass, Timpani, and Piano
"Fantasie" for B flat Clarinet, Bass Clarinet, and Orchestra
"Lawrence"–Clarinet Concerto
"Magnificat" for Strings, Piano, and Women's Chorus
"Our Town"–Overture for Orchestra
Piano Concerto Nos. 1 to 4
Piano Toccata
String Quartet Nos. 1 and 2
"The Troubadour" for Woodwind Quintet and Piano

Credential File Available
Placement Office
Mannes College of Music
140 Riverside Drive
New York, NY 10025

Hector Sanchez, musician

823 Lima Drive
Rio Valley, CA 94663
415/555-4877
H.Sanchez04@xxx.com

Performance Experience

Choral

- Rio Valley High School Mixed Choir (4 years)
- Rio Valley High School Boys Choir (2 years)
- Rio Valley High School Show Choir (3 years)
- Rio Valley High School Madrigal Chorus (2 years)

Band

- Rio Valley High School Orchestra
- Rio Valley High School Marching Band

Teaching Experience

- Echo Park Pro Musica (Redding, CA)
  Counselor, junior league
- Private studio—vocal coaching

Teachers

Voice: Trudy Berger, James Davidson
Trumpet: John Biggs
Piano: Mary Jane Howe

Awards

Rio Valley High School Music Achievement Award
Scholarship Recipient—Echo Park Pro Musica

References

Available upon request

JESSICA WU

333 E. Stadium Dr. • Kalamazoo, MI 49007
(616) 555-3735 • J.Wu@xxx.com

Height: 5'2"   Hair and Eyes: Brown
Weight: 130   Age Range Played: 12–35

MUSICAL THEATER

The Sound of Music, Maria, Kalamazoo Carr Theater
A Little Night Music, Anne, Western Michigan University
Little Shop of Horrors, Ronnette, WMU
Sweeney Todd, Joanna, WMU
Pippin, Catherine, Kalamazoo College

OPERA

The Elixer of Love, Adina, WMU
The Magic Flute, First Lady (Pamina cover), WMU
Cosi fan Tutte, Despina, WMU
The Impressario, Mme. Trillo, WMU

ROLES PREPARED

The Ballad of Baby Doe, Baby Doe, WMU
Manon, Manon, WMU
Der Rosenkavelier, Sophie, WMU
Don Giovanni, Zerlina, WMU

TRAINING

Teachers and Coaches:	Rose D'Angelou, Thomas Bickel, Libby Jonas
Acting:	Nancy Edelman, Paul Frisch
Dance:	Ballet, Jazz, Ballroom
Director:	Children's Theater, Kalamazoo Carr Theater
Instruments:	Piano, Guitar

EDUCATION

Western Michigan University, M.M. (Opera Performance), expected 2005
Western Michigan University, B.A. (Music Performance: Voice), 2003
Kalamazoo College Pre-College Music and Arts Program, 1995–1999

JEROME ANTHONY SMITH

221B Baker Street
Toledo, OH 43608
419-555-6259
jas@xxx.com

Hair: Brown
Eyes: Brown
Height: 6 ft. 2 in.
Weight: 180 lbs.

TEACHERS

Sergei Borga	Tucson, Arizona
Joi Nobel, Ty Hind	Pittsburgh, Pennsylvania
Esther Jing-Carr	Toledo, Ohio

PROFESSIONAL EXPERIENCE

1994–1997	Toledo Dance Co. corps de ballet	Director: Joshua Banks
1995–1996	Ballet Midwest corps de ballet	Director: Richard Rounder
1996–1998	Pennsylvania Ballet corps de ballet	Director: Benjamin George
1998–2001	Arizona Ballet corps de ballet	Director: Pasha Ronan
2001–2002	National Ballet soloist	Director: Henry Davison

Since 2002 I have maintained guest artist contracts with the following companies:

Utah Ballet	Director: Margo Vitrella
Portland City Ballet	Director: Marni Beaty
Houston Ballet	Director: Carl Heinreiksen
Pittsburgh Ballet	Director: Shari Thilson-Myer
Lake Erie Ballet	Director: Renee Rosen

SIGNIFICANT ACCOMPLISHMENTS

In 2003 I originated the role of Thomkin in Sergei Borga's ballet *Anatomy of a Nation*. Later that year I appeared in a photograhic essay of the production in *Dance Today*. I am featured in the short film *Dancin' Up to Heaven*, and I was interviewed for *Dance! America*, a documentary film commemorating the anniversary of the National Ballet Theatre. An original composition, *Life Without Wings*, was also featured in the film. This piece later received the Mar Award for Excellence.

REPERTOIRE

American Symphony	*Noel*
Carmina Burana	*Oiseau de l'Orange*
Cinderella	*Romeo and Juliet*
Firebird	*Rosa Lee*
Gigi	*Serenade*
La Jolite	*Sleeping Beauty*
Life Without Wings	*Swan Lake*
The Merry Widow	*Symphony in C*
The Nutcracker Suite	*Western Song*

TEACHING EXPERIENCE

Portland City Ballet	Portland, OR
Pittsburgh Ballet	Pittsburgh, PA
National Ballet Theatre	Washington, DC
Toledo Dance Company	Toledo, OH
Ballet Midwest	Dayton, OH
Arizona Regional Ballet	Tucson, AZ
Filbert Junior College	Filbert, UT
Austin Concert Ballet	Austin, TX
Arise Dance Theatre	Salt Lake City, UT
Utah Regional Ballet	Provo, UT

CHOREOGRAPHY

Life Without Wings	National Ballet Theatre
Allegro in D	Austin Concert Ballet

Natalie Herrera

3630 N. Greenview • Chicago, IL 60614
Home: (312) 555-2610 • Cellular: (312) 555-6466
E-mail: N.Herrera@xxx.com

Personal Information

Height: 5'2", Weight: 105 lbs., Hair and Eyes: dark brown

Training

Ballet
Lehmann School of Ballet, Chicago
Ruth Page School of Dance, Chicago
Howard Davis Studio, New York City
Jamb Chung Studio, New York City
Walter Raines, Alvin Alley School, New York City

Modern
Penny Paretsky, Ricardo Ribera Dance Etcetera, Chicago
Denise Jefferson Harper and Maria Bryant, Alvin Alley School

Jazz
Joel Hall, Joel Hall Studio, Chicago
Lou Conte, Hubbard Street Dance, Chicago
Martin Stone, Ed Sullivan Studios, New York City

Credits

Soloist, Joel Hall Dancers
Soloist, Ricardo Ribera Dance Etcetera
Soloist, Ballet Latina, New York City
Soloist, Lamplight Dinner Theatre, "That's Dancin'!"
Soloist, *Nutcracker*, "Danse Arabe," Highland Park Civic
Soloist, *Nutcracker*, corps de ballet, "Waltz of the Flowers," Lehmann School
Soloist, *Cinderella*, Lehmann School

Choreography

La Liaise, Maurice Ravel, Joel Hall, reviewed in *Dance Today*, June 1998
"Java Jive," Manhattan Transfer, jazz presentation
"Brazilian Nights," jazz solo, Ed Sullivan Studios
"Hot and Now," jazz review, Ricardo Ribera Dance Etcetera
Bloomfield Ballet, jazz dance workshop, Devin Diamanti, Bloomfield, IL
Westmont Ballet Studio, ballet workshop, Westmont, NJ

References

Available upon request

Laralynn Jennings

234 Mapletree Avenue
Baltimore, MD 21216
410-555-5478

Date of Birth: 6/3/82
Height: 5'4"

Education

B.F.A. in Dance with honors, University of Maryland, December 2004

Dance Experience

University of Maryland Dance Company

Don't Just Stand There (Tessa Michel)
Toucan Sam Tango (T. R. Jamison), duet
Give Me an "A" (Alan Bond)
To Misha, with Love (Rubix), Amor
Young Blood (Chinoo Patel)

American Dance Theatre

Stars and Stripes (Ballanchine)
Gigi (Lunaire), Gigi
Rodeo (Agnes de Mille)
The Nutcracker (Petipa), "Dance of the Reed Pipes"

Ontario Repertory Ballet

Cinderella (Petipa), Wicked Stepmother

Training

University of Maryland 2000-2004
Ballet: Mira Browning, Giselle Martinique
Modern: Bartholo Jenkins, Adam Coles, Jeannie Jones

Rosario Dance Studio 1993-2000
Ballet, Jazz, Tap, Modern, Character, and Mime

American Academy of Ballet Arts 1989-1993
Ballet: Alicia Doggett

Training (cont.)

Master Classes/Workshops

Ballet	Modern	Jazz
Cathy Burnett	Tory Spencer	Bobby Cort
Liza Greene	Alana Parsons	Tricia Latman
Darius Michaels	Sibarus Dean	
Joseph Pincus		

Teaching Experience (Beginner to Adult Advanced)

Dance Baltimore (2002-2004): Ballet and Jazz
Rosario Dance Studio (2000-2003): Ballet, Tap, Modern
Private teaching (2001-2004): Ballet, Modern, Tap, and Character

Scholarships/Awards

The Roosevelt Foundation Scholarship
The University of Maryland Foundation Scholarship
The Martina Zotto Scholarship (University of Maryland)
Washington School of the Arts Summer Program
Silver Spring School of Ballet Summer Program

References

Mira Browning
The University of Maryland
14 Brown Hall
Baltimore, MD 21208

Tessa Michel
The University of Maryland
14 Brown Hall
Baltimore, MD 21208

More available upon request

Michael Alan Pierce
french horn

145 Main Street #2
Bangor, ME 04322
(207) 555-3236
MAPierce@xxx.com

Objective

To continue the pursuit of a performance career in orchestral music by gaining admission to a well-respected music institution.

Experience

Orchestral

Peabody Symphony Orchestra - Principal	2001-2003
Peabody Symphony Orchestra - Assistant Principal	1999-2001
Peabody Mixed Brass Choir - Assistant Principal	1996-1999
Peabody Opera Orchestra - Principal	1997-2000

Chamber

Peabody Chamber Brass - Principal	1999-2003
Peabody Chamber Opera Orchestra	1997-1999

Awards

Peabody Achievement Award for Graduate Studies	2003
Peabody Concerto Competition - Second Place	2001
St. Stephens Episcopal Collegiate Scholarship	1996-1997

Teachers

Donna Burke - Principal, Portland Symphony	2000-Present
Kadim Shur - Peabody Conservatory of Music	1996-2000
Russell Lenhoff - Principal, Boston Lyric Opera	1993-1996

Education

Peabody Conservatory of Music - Baltimore, MD
Bachelor of Music in French Horn Performance, December 2003

Member

American Musicians Guild
American Brass Union
Phi Beta Kappa

Kenneth M. Shannon
flute

School Address
Marks Hall, Room 224
University of Colorado
Boulder, CO 80310
(303) 555-3120

Home Address
45 Long Avenue
Arlington, VA 22202
(703) 555-3574

Orchestral Experience
Professional
Boulder Summer Wind Quintet (Boulder, CO)
Arlington Civic Orchestra (Arlington, VA)

University of Colorado at Boulder
University Festival Orchestra
University Chamber Orchestra
University Winds

Other
All-State Orchestra (Richmond, VA)
Brandywine Music Camp (Brandywine, MD)
Taft High School Orchestra

Honors
Taft High School Concerto Competition, First Place
Lavoir Parent Music Achievement Award (two-year scholarship)

Private Teachers
Dana Goldberg, University of Colorado at Boulder (current teacher)
James Banner, Arlington Symphony Orchestra

Education
University of Colorado at Boulder School of Music
B. Mus. - Flute Performance
Degree expected in 2005

Taft High School of the Arts
Graduated June 2001

CAROL M. LOOMIS

85 Peace Drive
Portland, OR 97219
(503) 555-0186
C.Loomis@xxx.com

OBJECTIVE:

A part-time position as a dance instructor that will enable me to attend college classes while working with children.

EDUCATION:

June 2003 Graduate of Lakeside High School
Portland, OR
GPA 3.00/4.00

In fall 2003, I will begin attending Lewis and Clark College in Portland, OR.

WORK EXPERIENCE:

Assistant Dance Instructor
The Dance Studio, Portland, OR

Responsibilities: teaching tap and jazz to school-age children
Summers 2001, 2002

SPECIAL SKILLS:

Two-year member of 4-H Club
Four years Jazzercize
Six years tap and ballet lessons
Diligent and friendly dance instructor

REFERENCES:

Cathy Delude, Dance Instructor,
The Dance Studio
(503) 555-1154

Norman Haney, family friend
(503) 555-7600

Joshua K. Peck

301 Coates Drive • International Falls, MN 56649
Josh.Peck@xxx.com • (218) 555-2452

Objective:	To become an actor in a community theater.
Acting Experience:	Member of the Drama Club for four years.
Work Experience:	June 2003–present McDonald's Restaurant International Falls, MN Responsibilities: operate cash register, improve and maintain the site and lobby, cook, and close the restaurant at night. June 2002–August 2002 Taco Bell Restaurant International Falls, MN Responsibilities: operated electronic cash register, prepared and packaged food, and cleaned and maintained restaurant.
Personal:	Competed in track and field for six years. I was a multi-event winner and team captain my senior year. • Member of the football team in 2002 and 2003. • Fluent in written and conversational French.
Education:	Graduated from International Falls High School in 2003. • Planning to attend St. Cloud State University in St. Cloud, MN, in 2004. • Expected graduation date of 2008 with a major in Speech/Communication/Theater Education.
References:	Available upon request.

Daniel M. Redding

Present
222 Washington Ave.
Sommerville, MA 02181
617-555-1188

Permanent
400 E. LaSalle Dr.
Milwaukee, WI 53211
515-555-0212

Postgraduate studies, Boston University
Baccalaureate 2004, Boston University, Boston, MA
Matriculated 2000, Harvey Mudd School, Racine, WI

Assistant Stage Manager: Milwaukee Light Opera (2003 season)
- Managed the season run of two light opera and operetta productions.
- Assisted the stage manager in preparation for over forty other performances in the full season repertory.

Organist and Cantor: Grace Lutheran Church, Cedar Bluff, WI (1999–2000)
- Served as organist for weekly services and major festivals and holidays.
- Organized and participated in special services involving other professional and volunteer musicians.

Tenor Soloist, Substitute Organist, and Music Director: Canton Presbyterian Church, Canton, MA (2001–2004)
- Assisted in musical selection and preparation of professional (paid) quartet in which I sang tenor.
- Substituted for the director both as organist and conducting from the console.

Sales Representative: Milwaukee Symphony Chorus, Milwaukee, WI (Summers 2001–2002)
- Representative in telephone sales and ticket subscription renewal.
- Served as assistant coordinator of the phone drive.

Office Assistant: Boston University Admissions Office (September 2001–May 2004)
- General office work including reception, filing, word processing (Microsoft Word), and database programming (FileMaker Pro).

Chorister: Milwaukee Symphony Chorus, Boston University Choir, Boston University Singers, The Longy Chamber Singers, Boston University Opera Chorus, Grace Lutheran Choir, Canton Presbyterian Choir, Wisconsin Honors Chorus.

References furnished upon request

Marcus Babbitt, Pianist

77 Chambers Street
New York, NY 10007
(212) 555-9723

Concert Engagements

The Riverside Church (NYC)
The Rutgers Church (NYC)
Historical New York Tour (Various Locations)
SUNY at Binghampton Alumni Series (NY)
New York Athletic Club Series (NYC)
A Chorus Line (NYC)

Commercial Engagements

Forever Plaid
• Conductor/Pianist 2000–2002
• Music Director 2002–2003
• Chicago and Boston Tours
The Gondoliers (NYC)
West Side Story (NYC)

Chamber Music Engagements

Manhattan Chamber Orchestra
• Artistic Director 2001–present
• Concerts at schools and libraries throughout NYC and Long Island
• Conductors: Phillipe Bryere, Lance Matheson, Jeremy Dietz

Education

Manhattan School of Music, Master of Music, 2001
SUNY at Binghampton, Bachelor of Fine Arts, 1999

Principal Teachers

Piano: Everett Harding, Joshua Barr, Loren Biggs
Master Classes: Jeremy Dietz, Alan Loeber, Timothy Kelly

Credential File Available
Manhattan School of Music
Office of Placement Services
120 Claremont Avenue
New York, NY 10027

Lestor Lyons, Tenor

456 Chicago Ave.
Chicago, IL 60613
Lestor.Lyons@xxx.com
(312) 555-2277

Height: 5′6″
Weight: 150
Hair/Eyes: Brown

Opera Roles

Nemorino, *L'Elisir D'Amor*, Northeastern Illinois Opera
Gastone, *La Traviata*, Northeastern Illinois Opera
Don Ottavio, *Don Giovanni*, Northeastern Illinois Opera
Tamino, *Die Zauberflöte*, Northeastern Illinois Opera
Nankipoo, *The Mikado*, Northeastern Illinois Opera
Detleffe, *The Student Prince*, Northeastern Illinois Opera

Roles Studied

Don Ottavio, *Don Giovanni*, Northeastern Illinois
Tenor, *Postcard from Morocco*, Northeastern Illinois
Le Pecheaurs de Perles, *Nadir*, Northeastern Illinois
Falstaff, *Fenton*, Northeastern Illinois

Oratorio/Concert

Soloist, *Messiah*, Northeastern Symphony
Soloist, *Ninth Symphony*, Chicago Civic Opera
Soloist, *A Night of Mozart*, Elgin Art League

Teachers

Loren Jennings (current), James Steubin, Penny Christian

Coaches/Directors

Eric Lieber, Jonathan Hull, Diane Mosley, Leonardo Morales,
Jocylin DeBeers

Education

B.M. Voice Performance, Northeastern Illinois University
(degree expected in 2005)
Grand Lake Summer Institute, Grand Lake, WI (2003)

Elizabeth Moss, Soprano

2347 N. Oak St. • Lake Forest, IL 60604
Beth.Moss@xxx.com • (847) 555-5010

Opera Performances

Donna Anna, *Don Giovanni*, Skylight Opera Theater
Violetta, *La Traviata*, Northwestern University Opera
Arminda, *La Finta Giardiniera*, Northwestern University Opera
Desdemona, *Otello*, Northwestern University Opera
Fiordiligi, *Cosi fan Tuttei*, Risotto Festival

Concert Performances

Ein Deutsches Requiem, Brahms, Toledo Symphony
Messiah, Handel, Northwestern University
Missa Solemnis, Beethoven, Northwestern University
Mass in C Minor, Mozart, St. James Cathedral
Gloria, Vivaldi, St. James Cathedral
Messiah, Handel, South Bend Choir

Future Engagements

Leonore, *Fidelio*, Skylight Opera
Ein Deutsches Requiem, Brahms, Springfield Symphony

Awards and Honors

Siobbhan M. Horowitz Grant, 2004
Pi Lambda Nu, National Music Sorority, inducted 2000

Education and Training

Master of Music in Voice Performance, Northwestern University, in progress
Bachelor of Music in Music Education, Northwestern University, 2000

Voice: Nancy Burns Mayer, Elizabeth Crenshaw, Robert Hays
Coaches: Jordan Bonnerman, Alice Keeler, Joanne Lotti, Nathan Lowe

GEOFF BERMAN   708-555-2480

15901 Oak Park Ave.
Tinley Park, IL 60477

Eligible Performer/EMC
Voice: Baritone
Ht: 5'9" Wt: 140
Hair: Brown Eyes: Green

THEATER

Wait Until Dark, Harry, Lighthouse Theatre
The Merry Wives of Windsor, Pistol, New Shakespeare Co.
Comedy of Errors, Dronio of Ephesus, New Shakespeare Co.
Devil's Advocate (Midwest Premiere), Luke, Nova Productions
Daylight Losings, Jimmy Dean, Lighthouse Theatre

MUSICAL THEATER

Fiddler on the Roof, Motel Kamzoil, Drury Lane Theatre
The Fantasticks, Mortimer, Playhouse Productions
Threepenny Opera, Beggar, Playhouse Productions
Grease, Sonny, Lakeshore Theatre
Annie, Rooster, Lakeshore Theatre

CHILDREN'S THEATER

Sleeping Beauty, Bad Stepdad, Kids Klub Productions
Snow White and the 7 Dudes, Narly, Kids Klub Productions
Hansel and Gretel, Owen the Wise Owl, abc Playhouse
The Adventures of Pooh, Roo, abc Playhouse

FILM/TELEVISION

Cobb, Player #5, Columbia Pictures
The Watchtower, Reporter, Universal Studios
Home Alone 2, Store Clerk, Hughes Entertainment
Monkey Business, Newspaper Man, Fox Entertainment
The Cutting Room Floor, Waiter, CinemaScope
The Ann Davis Story, Hotel Patron, Home Box Office
One Night Only, Guest Artist, Chicago Cable

INDUSTRIAL FILMS/COMMERCIALS

Jewel-Osco, Crown Communications
W. W. Grainger, in-house
Chicago Sun-Times, Don Harper Productions
Burger King, Franklin-Goode

TRAINING

Private voice lessons, Rudolph Glick
Acting, James Olin

WORKSHOPS

On-Camera, Duncan James
Mime, USC Mime Co.

SPECIAL SKILLS AND INTERESTS

Most dialects, improv, stage combat, technical theater, director, producer

Via Martinez

24 Seagull
Wilmington, NC 28402
(910) 555-0835
v.martinez@xxx.com

Roles

Don Pasquale, Norina, UNC Opera Theater
Don Giovanni, Zerlina, UNC Opera Theater
The Marriage of Figaro, Barbarina, UNC Opera Theater
The Fantasticks, Luisa, UNC Theater
Threepenny Opera, Lucy, UNC Theater
The Glass Menagerie, Laura, UNC Little Theater

Choral Experience

OPERA
Cosi fan Tutte
The Gondoliers
Ruddigore
Sweeney Todd

ENSEMBLE
UNC Choral Union
UNC Chamber Singers
Greensboro Baroque
Bernini Trio

Education

University of North Carolina at Greensboro
B.A. Liberal Arts

Voice: Raquel Lane, Dawn Hyde-Pierce, Susan Nix
Acting: Carrie Berg, John Berwyn, Daniel James
Dance: Lana Derring, Barb Jackson, Aron Theopholis

DEBORAH BENNETT
Mezzo-Soprano

31737 Tappen Hills Road
Tippicanoe, OH 44699
740-555-2592

OPERA

Rigoletto, Giovanna, Cleveland Opera
Carmen, Mercedes, Reed Dinner Theater
The Ballad of Baby Doe, Augusta, Ohio University Opera
Candide, Baroness (cover), Ohio University Players
La Traviata, Flora, Ohio University Opera
Suor Angelica, Monitor, Ohio University Opera

CONCERT

Elijah, Mendelssohn, Toledo Symphony
Requiem, Verdi, Wooster Chorus
Magnificat, Bach, Ohio University Collegium
Messiah, Handel, Reed Baroque Ensemble
Ninth Symphony, Beethoven, Toledo Festival Chorus

MUSICAL THEATER

The Phantom of the Opera, Madame Giry, Reed Playhouse
Sweeney Todd, Mrs. Lovett, Reed Playhouse
A Little Night Music, Charlotte, Wooster Repertory Theater
The Mikado, Katisha, Toledo Savoyards

EDUCATION

B.F.A., Ohio University, 1999
Certificate in Vocal Studies, Toledo Conservatory, 2004

Beatrice Young

Mezzo-Soprano

4501 West Mill Road • Grosse Pointe, MI 48072
B.Young@xxx.com • 313/555-1234

"Ms. Young's voice was beautiful . . . with luster throughout the range."
—Detroit Press

"technically polished and dramatically secure"
—The Sentinel (Michigan)

Opera
Carmen, Mercedes, Michigan Light Opera
Carmen, Mercedes, Toledo Opera
The Marriage of Figaro, Cherubino, University of Michigan
Die Fledermaus, Prince Orlofsky, Michigan Light Opera
The Magic Flute, Second Lady, University of Michigan
Dido and Aeneas, Dido, University of Michigan
Amahl and the Night Visitors, Mother, University of Michigan

Oratorio/Concert Engagements
"A Night at the Opera," Detroit Symphony
Magnificat in D, Windham Symphony Chorale
Vesperae Solemnes, Windham Symphony
Messiah, University of Michigan
Messiah, Hargrove College

Awards/Honors
Metropolitan Opera Auditions, Regional Finalist, Great Lakes Region (1995)
Madeline T. Jenson Opera Award, Winner, Grosse Pointe, MI (1994)
Metropolitan Opera Auditions, District Finalist, Detroit, MI (1993)

Training
M.M., University of Michigan
B.M., University of Michigan

Teachers/Coaches
Elizabeth Allen, Jonathan Long, Suzanne Ziebler, Robert Plante, James Norton

• XIAN LEE •

Percussion

282 Green Street • Jamaica Plain, MA 02117
Xian.Lee@xxx.com • (617) 555-5633

• TRAINING

Jonathan Pressman, New England Conservatory of Music
September 2001–May 2003

Michael Lawrence, Berkley School of Music
June 2003–December 2003

Patricia Stone-Berry, Wellesley Philharmonic Orchestra
1995–2001

• PERFORMANCE EXPERIENCE

- Boston Lyric Opera Orchestra, October 2003–April 2004
- Wellesley Symphony Orchestra, May 2002–present
- NEC Orchestra, September 2001–May 2003
- NEC Contemporary Ensemble, September 2001–May 2003
- NEC Wind Ensemble, September 2002–May 2003

• AWARDS

- Pi Kappa Lambda, May 2003
- New England Conservatory 20th Century Achievement Prize, 2003
- Doris B.Yates Percussion Competition, East Coast Region, 2nd place, June 2002
- New England Artists Guild Concerto Competition, 1998

• EDUCATION

- New England Conservatory of Music, M.M., May 2003
- B.A., Wellesley College, May 2001

GRETCHEN REICHMANN

School
11 Cherry Lane Blvd.
Peachtree, GA 30321
404-555-3392

Home
233 Delancy St.
Philadelphia, PA 02114
515-555-1451

OBJECTIVE
A position teaching strings and/or general music at the elementary or secondary level.

EDUCATION
University of Georgia, May 2002.
B.A. in Music Education with String emphasis.

EXPERIENCE
Atlanta Public Schools, Atlanta, GA
Taught strings, band, orchestra, and general music to seventh through twelfth graders; prepared students for performance.

Philadelphia Public Schools, Philadelphia, PA
Worked as a substitute teacher specializing in general music at the middle, junior high, and high school levels.

City of Philadelphia Parks District
Taught general music and art at Summer Youth Program; prepared students for weekly talent shows.

Bright Days Kid's Center
Assisted preschool teacher; taught music classes; led singing; general duties as preschool teacher.

Performance Experience
Summer music festivals, 1997-2002; Senior recital, 2001; University String Ensemble, 2000-2002.

Travel
Toured Russia with Youth Chamber Orchestra at Temple University, summer 1996.

Professional Affiliations
Member of the national Music Education Conference, American String Teachers Association, and Georgia State Music Educators Association.

CARY T. CHRISTIAN

24 Pawnee Valley Road • Brockport, NY 14420
CTChristian@xxx.com • 716-555-8102

OBJECTIVE	To teach general music (K-8) or choral music (9-12) in a challenging and progressive school setting.
EDUCATION	Eastman School of Music, May 2004 Bachelor of Music in Music Education and Organ Performance New York State 4-Year Provisional Certification: Music, K-12
TEACHING EXPERIENCE	**Mount Vernon United Methodist Church, Vernon Hills, Indiana** **Assistant Children's Choir Director/Organist, 1998-2000** – Accompanied performances of Children's Choir during Sunday services. – Assisted in choosing appropriate sacred repertoire for young voices. – Prepared choir in director's absence. **Sunday School Teacher, 1997-1998** **King Elementary School** **Rochester School District** **Student Teacher, Spring 2002** – Assisted in teaching two choral ensembles, 5th and 6th grades. – Assisted with general music, K-6. **Roosevelt High School** **Tutor, Music and Algebra, 2000-2002** **United Methodist Midwest Arts Camp, Hammond, Indiana** **Staff Accompanist and Music Leader, 1996-1999** **Camp Counselor, 1995-1997**

RELATED EXPERIENCE

Eastman Madrigal Chorus
Director, 2002-2004

Eastman Community Chorus
Assistant Choir Director, 2001-2004

Eastman Choral Union
Student Accompanist/Tenor Section Leader, 2001-2004

Eastman Gilbert and Sullivan Players
Music Director/Conductor for various shows, 2001-2004

KEYBOARD EXPERIENCE

Eastman School of Music, Rochester, New York
– Studied organ with Douglas Bing and Roger Stanford.
– Studied piano with Roger Graham.
– Studied harpsichord with Margaret Chase Lindbergh.
– Accompanied vocalists and instrumentalists in approximately ten recitals yearly.
– Participated in keyboard master classes with Leonard Rudolph and Carter Lehman.

Ten years of piano studies with Alisa Jeffries, 1990-2000

AWARDS

Lisette Pressman Scholarship, 2003
Excellence in musicianship and teaching ability

Indiana State Scholastic Achievement Award, 2000

PROFESSIONAL AFFILIATIONS

American Choral Directors Association
American Guild of Organists
Music Educators National Conference

A R M O N D O   B A N D E R A
Viola

55 Fresno Drive   A.Bandera@xxx.com
Santa Fe, NM 87518   (505) 555-2674

O B J E C T I V E

To continue to perform the viola while actively pursuing a teaching career in the field of music history.

P E R F O R M A N C E   E X P E R I E N C E

- Santa Fe Opera
- New Mexico Symphony
- Santa Fe Philharmonic—Substitute
- Santa Fe Conservatory Orchestra—Principal
- Santa Fe Christian College String Quartet—Founder

F E S T I V A L S

- Spoleto Music Festival
- Nordstrom International Festival, Sweden
- Bloom Lake Music Festival (Bloom Lake, OR)
- Canadian-American String Quartet Program, Vancouver, BC

E D U C A T I O N

Santa Fe Conservatory of Music: Master of Music (2003)
- Music History and Theory

Santa Fe Christian College (1991)
- Bachelor of Arts in History
  Minor in Viola Performance

Teachers: James Hendricks, Pia Herada
Coaches: Lane Myer, Penny Chase, Leonard Lewin

TEACHING EXPERIENCE

History Department, Santa Fe Conservatory
• Teaching Assistant/Lecturer

Spring Park Public Schools (Spring Park, NM)
• Tutor: Social Studies, General Music

Adams College Musical Extension Program (Santa Fe)
• Private studio, viola

NOTABLE ACHIEVEMENTS

Publications:

"Richard Strauss: Creativity in Adversity"
• Master's Thesis, Published in *Music History Monthly* in November 2003.

"A History Lesson: Teaching Children the Value of Music"
• Lecture prepared for presentation at Music Educators of the West Conference, June 2003. Published in Annual Report.
• To be revised and reprinted in *Musical America* in 2004.

I am currently preparing a series of lectures concerning the lack of adequate music history curriculum in secondary schools.

Barbara Hines Johnson   *Harpist*

435 W. 88th St., Apt. 5

New York, NY 10025

Home: 212-555-2245

Cellular: 212-555-8131

Orchestra Engagements

New York Philharmonic, 2002-present
New Jersey Philharmonic, 2000-present
New Jersey Symphony, 1999-2000
Hartford Philharmonic (CT), 1996-1997
Tanglewood Festival Orchestra, 1995-1996
Westmont Orchestra (MA), 1995-1998
Woodstock Philharmonic, 1994-1995

Opera Engagements

New York City Opera
Bronx Opera
Pocket Opera (NY)
New York Gilbert and Sullivan Players

Musical Theatre

She Loves Me (Broadway)
Starlight Express (Broadway)
Jesus Christ Superstar
The King and I
Bye Bye Birdie

Education

Mannes College of Music
Master of Music, 2000

New England Conservatory
Bachelor of Music, 1998

Tufts University
Bachelor of Arts with Honors, 1998

Principal Teachers

Nina Lang-Schultz (Principal, New Jersey Philharmonic)
Harold Thiessen (Principal, New York City Opera)
Jeanette McPhail (Principal, Boston Symphony Orchestra)

Reviews

"She's fantastic—a real find!"   *—New York Post*

"[Ms. Hines] played with great skill and musicality . . ."   *—Boston Globe*

"Virtuosity and beauty of tone were among the talents exhibited by the young Ms. Hines in her triumphant debut recital . . ."   *—New York Daily News*

". . . a lively performance . . . full of pizzazz."   *—New Jersey Sentinel*

"Ms. Hines Johnson captivated the audience with brilliant playing and an innate sensitivity to the music."   *—Hartford Monitor*

Louise O'Shea

Dancer – Choreographer – Teacher
704 Hennepin Avenue
Minneapolis, MN 55403
(612) 555-3340

Performing Credits

Stage
- Soloist and Senior Member of JazzHot Inc., a National Touring Company. Artistic Directors: Lucie and Tag Hawkins.
- Freddy Fargo's "World of Jazz Dance 2004"–Chicago.
- "JADE Review '03."
- "JADE Review '02."

Movies
- *The Red Shoes*. Director: Donna Pescow. Choreographer: Judith Jamison. Touchstone Pictures.
- *All That Glitters* (made for cable). Director: Matt Spielberg. Cinemax Studios.
- *Fame*. Director: Alan Parker. Paramount Pictures.
- *Never Give Up: The Josie Johnson Story* (made for TV). Director: David Rosen.

Choreography
- The Spring Dance (annual dance concert, 3 years) - University of Santa Barbara, Santa Barbara, CA.
- "JADE Review '00 - Malibu, CA.
- "Golden Hollywood" (musical review) 2001 - USB.

Training

Jazz
- Lucie and Tag Hawkins
- Bennett DuBonn
- Freddie Fargo

Ballet
- Juliette Mitchell
- Steven Woo

Teaching Credits

- Head of jazz department at Bob Fosse School for the Performing Arts in Minneapolis, MN, as well as instructor at three other local dance academies.

- Independent Choreographer–Dance Instructor for Crane High School in Malibu, CA, for three years (1999-2002).

- Dance Instructor at the highly competitive Red Hill Summer Dance Program, West Redding, CA.

- Dance-Movement Instructor and Assistant Director at Gymbunnies Children's Gym in Los Angeles, CA.

- Jazz-Movement Instructor for children at four private studios and academies in the Twin Cities.

- Dance Instructor and Choreographer for dance groups throughout Los Angeles including Fox Studios and Dance Academy of the West.

- Master classes taught throughout the United States.

LAUREN DE FIGLIO, BASSOON

24 Mill Road
New Rockport, NY 12560
(914) 555-2464
ldefiglio@xxx.com

∽ EDUCATION
Oberlin Conservatory of Music: Oberlin, Ohio
B.M. in Bassoon Performance/B.A. in Biology
GPA: 3.62/4.00
Date of Graduation: May 2003

∽ PROFESSIONAL ORCHESTRAL EXPERIENCE
Akron Symphony Orchestra (Akron, OH): principal
Brooklyn Opera Theater Orchestra (Brooklyn, NY): 2nd
Rockport Chamber Ballet (Rockport, NY): principal and 2nd

∽ OTHER ORCHESTRAL EXPERIENCE
Oberlin Orchestra: principal and 2nd
Oberlin Wind Ensemble: 2nd
Oberlin Opera Theater Orchestra: principal
MENC East Coast Orchestra: principal and 2nd
New York All-State Orchestra: associate principal

∽ CHAMBER MUSICAL EXPERIENCE
Oberlin Winter Term Woodwind Quintet, Midwest Tour
Oberlin Woodwind Quintet "Zephyr"
Oberlin Chamber Winds

∽ AWARDS AND HONORS
Lindberg Chamber Music Competition, finalist
New York All-State Scholarship Competition
Pi Kappa Lambda

∽ TEACHERS AND OTHER REFERENCES
Robert Jernigan, Professor of Bassoon, Oberlin Conservatory
Caline Mills, Professor of Orchestral Conducting, Oberlin Conservatory
Luis Garcia-Cortes, Conductor, MENC, East Coast Conservatory

PAMELA GIUFFRE
actress/model

1120 N. King Rd. • Detroit, MI 43020 • p.giuffre@xxx.com • (616) 555-6647

Height: 5'8"
Weight: 106
Hair: Blonde
Eyes: Hazel

Television Commericals
Bounty
Career Barbie
EZ Waterbeds
Luvs
McDonald's
Mom's Pickles
Pringles Potato Chips

Film/Industrial Promotions
Michigan Bell
Wendy's
Bessie: A Mule (short film)

Print Modeling
House & Garden
JC Penney
Leeds Inc.
Sears

Coaches and Related Experience
Acting: Nonnie Owens, Theo Barnett
Improv: Zack Coen
Modeling: Lara Webb Talent
Dance: 6 years ballet/modern: 2 years tap, 2 years jazz
Training: Grosse Pointe Performing Arts Center: 5 summers
Member: Young Artists Studio (Detroit, MI): 4 years

Luisa Katarina Gerasimo

Tap, Jazz, Modern, Ballet

3105 West Monroe Avenue
Fairbanks, OH 53422
E-mail: L.Gerasimo@xxx.com
Cellular: 413/555-9436

Professional Objective

To obtain a full-time position teaching dance/movement in a primary or secondary
school. Willing to relocate.

Experience

Dance/Aerobics Instructor, September 2002 to Present
Pleasant Valley Adult Education - Pleasant Valley, Ohio

- Plan and teach 10 class sessions per week, with 15 to 20 students per class.
- Demonstrate and lead exercise sequences to stretch, tone, and condition
  participants.
- Teach students to monitor their heart rates, estimate their body-fat percentages,
  and set realistic health goals.

Creative Movement Specialist, January 2000 to September 2002
Dayton Daycare - Dayton, Ohio

- Developed class plans for hour-long sessions with 20 toddlers twice a week.
- Taught age appropriate movement, dance, and exercise.

Team Teacher, February 1999 to December 1999
Marigold Child Development Center - Dayton, Ohio

- Taught and team-taught primary students with physical disabilities (all subject
  areas, including physical education).
- Worked with other teachers and development specialists to ensure activities and
  curriculum were accessible to all students, regardless of their individual abilities.

Page 1 of 2

Education

B.A. in Physical Education, Ohio State University
• Emphasis on physiological development in children.

Dayton Adult Education
• Course work in nutrition and health in adolescent and adult populations; active participant in adult women's volleyball and basketball leagues.

Certification

• Multiple-subject teaching credential.
• Certified Jazzercise instructor.

References

Available upon request.

JOSHUA LIEBER   CLARINETIST

410 St. Botoph Street, #3
Boston, MA 02116
(617) 555-9504
J.Lieber@xxx.com

EDUCATION

NEW ENGLAND CONSERVATORY OF MUSIC
Boston, MA
Bachelor of Music, May 2004

TRAINING

PRINCIPAL TEACHERS
David Wrightwood
Laurence Pauling

MASTER CLASSES
Mimi Cohen
Sam Everding

CHAMBER MUSIC COACHES
Carl Evans
James Brody
Helen Jarrett

PERFORMANCE EXPERIENCE

SOLO APPEARANCE
Seattle Youth Orchestra
December 2002

ORCHESTRAL
New England Conservatory Orchestra
Harvard University Orchestra
Longy School Orchestra

RECITALS
Senior Recital, January 2004
Boston 4-H Club, February 2004
NEC Contemporary Ensemble, May 2003

REFERENCES   Available upon request

■ DORIE JOHNSON, Composer

1289 Carter Road ■ Montgomery, AL 36112
205/555-8573 ■ D.Johnson@xxx.com

■ EDUCATION

University of Alabama School of Liberal and Performing Arts
M.M., Composition/Music Technology
B.S., Mathematical Studies

■ TEACHERS

Composition: Eileen Handy, Frederick Pincus
Music Technology: Jackson Hauser, Roger Klein, Darnell Wilson, Margaret Donalson
Piano: Jacques Brodin, Judith Goodwin
Voice: Camila McHugh, Taran Redding-Gagne, Jay Dumanian

■ ADDITIONAL AREAS OF STUDY

Music: Aural Skills, Chamber Music, Music History and Theory, UA Choral Union
Liberal Arts: Women's Studies, American History, Mathematics

■ WORKS PERFORMED

Piano Trio No. 2 for Cello and Electric Bass, University Hall
"Montgomery, 1968" for Tape and String Quartet, University Hall
"Stormfront" Fantasy for Wind Choir and Tape, Honors Recital

■ ADDITIONAL COMPOSITIONS (Partial List)

MIDI Mini-Concerto for Synthesizer and Orchestra String Quartet for Electric Strings
"I Wandered Lonely as a Cloud" Cantata for Voice and Synthesizer
Graduation Theme for Brass Quintet and Men's Chorus (composed for student film short)
Piano Trio No. 1
Piano Solos Nos. 1-8

■ MEMBERSHIPS

American Composers Workshop
Women Composers of America

Kristina Podowlski, Conductor/Coach

82 Sidell Avenue, Apt. 5D • Long Island City, NY 11102 • (718) 555-4512

Conductor	**Opera/Musical Theater** Bel Canto Opera Theater (NYC), Founder Brooklyn Opera Theater, Conductor Village Opera Theater, Music Director New York Gilbert & Sullivan Co., Music Director Opera New York, Assistant Music Director Trenton Opera (NJ), Cover Conductor **Orchestra** Bronx Chamber Players, Assistant Conductor Boro Chamber Orchestra, Guest Conductor Wildwood Music Festival, Student Orchestra
Coach	**Opera/Musical Theater** Opera Works Manhattan Civic Theater (Kalamazoo, MI) Wildwood Chamber Opera (NY) **Choral** Second Avenue Y Children's Choir (NYC) Riverside Church Senior Choir (NYC) Riverside Church Women's Chorale **Dance** Jamie Chung Studio (NYC) Ann Arbor School of Ballet (MI) University of Michigan Dance Classes (Ballet, Jazz, Modern)
Orchestra	**Viola** Ann Arbor Chamber Players Kalamazoo Civic Orchestra University of Michigan Symphony Orchestra University of Michigan Opera Orchestra
Education	Manhattan School of Music, M.M., 1999 University of Michigan, B.Mus., 1996

Seminars	The Conductors Studio (NYC)
	Arthur Fiedler Festival at Weston (MA)
	Wildwood Music Festival

Repertoire

Opera
Bizet, *Carmen*
Britten, *Peter Grimes*
Donizetti, *Don Pasquale* and *The Elixer of Love*
Gounod, *Romeo et Juliette*
Menotti, *The Consul* and *The Medium*
Mozart, *Cosi fan Tutte, The Magic Flute,* and
    The Marriage of Figaro
Offenbach, *The Tales of Hoffman*
Puccini, *La Boheme* and *Madama Butterfly*
Strauss, *Die Fledermaus*
Verdi, *Falstaff* and *La Traviata*

Musical/Operetta
Bernstein, *West Side Story*
Gilbert and Sullivan, *HMS Pinafore, Iolanthe,* and
    The Pirates of Penzance
Loesser, *Guys and Dolls*
Schmidt, *The Fantasticks*

Orchestra
Adams, *Harmonium*
Bach, *Brandenburg Concerto No. 2* and *Magnificat*
Barber, *Adagio for Strings*
Beethoven, *Ninth Symphony*
Brahms, *Symphonies No. 3, 4*
Copeland, *Appalachian Spring*
Faure, *Requiem*
Mozart, *Clarinet Concerto, Eine Kleine Nachtmusik,*
    Overture to Cosi fan Tutte, Overture to Don
    Giovanni, Overture to The Magic Flute, and
    Overture to the Marriage of Figaro
Schubert, *Unfinished Symphony*
Stravinsky, *L'Histoire du Soldat*

Natalie Coleman-Barnes, Soprano

4721 6th Avenue #3
Brooklyn, NY 11215
(718) 555-9201
N.Barnes@xxx.com

❧ OPERA ❧

Anne Truelove	*The Rake's Progress*
Countess	*The Marriage of Figaro*
Helena	*A Midsummer Night's Dream*
Liu	*Turandot*
Fiordiligi	*Cosi fan Tutte*
Amelia	*A Masked Ball*

❧ CONCERT ❧

Orff	*Carmina Burana*
Mozart	*Mass in C Minor*
Mahler	*Symphony No. 4*
Beethoven	*Ninth Symphony*

❧ EDUCATION/AWARDS ❧

San Francisco Conservatory of Music
Juilliard School of Music
Tulsa Opera Center for Young Artists
Liederkrantz Award Winner
Arlene Auger Foundation Winner
AGMA Member

"Natalie Coleman-Barnes lit up the stage with effortless singing and a commanding presence."
—Marc Leighton, *Opera Review*

MICHAEL SUTHERLAND

2757 Dolphin Drive • Arnold, MD 21012
(301) 555-5390 • M.Sutherland@xxx.com

EDUCATION

- UCLA School of Theater, Film and TV, September 2002 to present
  Comprehensive Major: Directing and Theater Management

- Arnold High School, September 1998 to June 2002
  Forensics Competitive Speech Team, 4 years
  Drama and Musical Productions, 3 years

AWARDS

- Bank of Maryland Fine Arts Award – 2nd place Region Finals
  Scholarship, 2002
- Veterans of Foreign Wars Speech Award, 2001 and 2002
- Student of the Year – Arnold High School, 2001
- State Forensics for Thematic Interpretation – 21st place (pieces included
  Torch Song Trilogy, *Into the Woods*, *Brighton Beach Memoirs*, and *Measure for Measure*), 2001
- Rotary Speech Award, 1998 and 1999
- Walter Johnson Musical Comedy Award at Anne Arundel Community
  Stage, 1999

PERFORMANCE THEATER EXPERIENCE

- Director, Collaborator, and Performer – AIDS Teen Theater, 2002
- Billy Crocker – *Anything Goes*, 2001
- Vincentio – *Taming of the Shrew*, 2001
- Albert – *Bye Bye Birdie*, 2000
- Frank Butler – *Annie Get Your Gun*, 1999
- Charlie – *Charlie and the Chocolate Factory*, 1999
- Ed – *You Can't Take It with You*, 1999
- Writer and Performer – AIDS Teen Theater, 1998 and 1999

TECHNICAL AND MANAGING THEATER EXPERIENCE

Anne Arundel Community Stage
- Production Assistant – *Fiddler on the Roof*, 2001
- Assistant Stage Manager – *Into the Woods*, 2000
- Chorus and Stage Hand – *Evita*, 1998
- Stage Hand – *My Fair Lady*, 1999

Peace Child
- Assistant Stage Manager, Props Assistant, 1998
- Assistant Technical Director, USA/USSR Production, 1998

Francis Luis Caracal

1415 North Gable Lane #3

Santa Fe, NM 87507

(505) 555-5521

E-mail: Fran.Caracal@xxx.com

Career Objective

To utilize my talent as a versatile and energetic professional dancer with experience in ballet, modern, and jazz dance.

Education

B.F.A., University of Oregon, 2000
Eugene, Oregon

Experience

2000-2004
- Performed with the Santa Fe Ballet under the direction of Jan Biltmore and Roy Haggen.
- Performed with Ballet Concertante, Santa Fe, New Mexico, under the direction of William Forester.
- Performed as a guest soloist with Portland City Ballet, Portland, Oregon.
- Performed as a guest soloist with San Antonio Dance Theater under the direction of Nanette DeSoto.

2000-2002
- Toured internationally as a member of Houston Ballet under the direction of Carl Henrieksen.

2000
- Performed with the Oregon Jazz Dance Factory under the direction of Martha Hough.

1996-1999
- Member of New Mexico Metropolitan Company.
- Studied with Prima Ballerina Ina Esteves of El Studio de Danza Moderna, Mexico City.

Choreography

2003-2004   Danz Santa Fe
2001-2003   Different Drummer Rhythm Dances
2001-2004   Changing Seasons
1996-2001   Choreographed for University of Oregon

Teaching

- Master Classes at Santa Fe Conservatory of Dance
- Master Classes for Oregon Jazz Dance Factory

Danza
- Instructed ballet and modern classes at El Studio de Moderna, Mexico City.
- Experience with teaching children at El Studio de Moderna and Portland City Ballet.

MARK REYNOLDS
TENOR

1212 Elm Avenue
South Bend, IN 46001
(812) 555-2278

Height: 5'10"
Weight: 185
Birthday: 8/1/79

OPERA ROLES

Spoletta	*Tosca*	Wildwood Festival
Gastone	*La Traviata*	Western Illinois Opera
Belfiore	*La Finta Giardiniera*	Western Illinois Opera
Detleffe	*The Student Prince*	Indiana Summer Repertory
Tamino	*Die Zauberflöte*	Indiana College

SCENES PERFORMED

Don Ottavio (Act I)	*Don Giovanni*	South Shore Opera
Nadir (Duet with Zurga)	*Le Pêcheurs de Perles*	Western Illinois Opera
Fenton (Act II, Scene 2)	*Falstaff*	Western Illinois Opera

ORATORIO/CONCERT

Soloist: *Messiah*	Orchestra Indiana
Soloist: *Beethoven's Ninth Symphony*	Bloomington Symphony
Soloist: Mozart *Requiem*	St. John's Church, Chicago
Soloist: "Basically Bach"	Illinois Arts League

TEACHERS/CONDUCTORS/COACHES

Elizabeth Randall (present), Martin Long, Jerry Appleton, Lois Whey,
Leonard Baum, Joseph Stewart, Elaine McEnroe, Lottie Harris

OPERA TRAINING/DIRECTORS

Stephen Ross, Dolores Dunne, James Magee, Stuart Lapin

EDUCATION

M.M. Vocal Performance: Western Illinois University, 2002
B.M. Music Education: Indiana Musical College, 1999

REFERENCES

Available upon request

LIZA GOLDMAN

1456 WEST ADDISON STREET • CHICAGO, IL 60613
(312) 555-9290 • L.GOLDMAN@XXX.COM

HEIGHT: 5'9" • WEIGHT: 145 • HAIR: AUBURN • EYES: GREEN

VOICE-OVER

America Online	Today's Woman
New England Telephone	General Nutrition Centers
Ameritech	Speedy Printers
New Jersey Bagel Company	EZ-Rest Mattress & Bedding
Century 21	Schaumburg Cadillac
Peppers Waterbeds	Dan DeSesto Oldsmobile
Chicago Cable Company	Ravenswood St. John's Hospital

INDUSTRIAL

Burger King – In-house
Chicago Cable Company – GBH Productions

COMMERCIAL

Walgreens – Roundup Productions
CashStation – L. B. Jameson & Company
Home Depot – Mara/Weiss Films

THEATER

As You Like It	Audrey	Goodman Theater
Mother Courage and Her Children	Ensemble	Halsted Theater Centre
A Midsummer Night's Dream	Moth	Chicago Shakespeare Co.
The Merry Wives of Windsor	Mrs. Page	Chicago Shakespeare Co.
Sad Dreams, Mad Dreams (Premiere)	Miss Star Cross	Moondog Theater

TRAINING

B.A. in Theater	Northwestern University, Chicago, Illinois
Acting:	Nora Goldman, Harold Leeds, Florence Kahn, James O'Malley
One Camera:	John Burns, Leo Watson, Terry Jonas
Dance:	Includes 4 years ballet, 2 years modern, 3 years jazz and tap

SPECIAL SKILLS

Fluent in Spanish; Conversational in Italian
Dialects: Standard British, American Southern, New England American
Gymnastics, Softball, Aerobics

GABRIELA PETERS
Soprano

240 W. 53rd St., #5B
New York, NY 10001
(212) 555-2274
www.GabrielaPeters.com

OPERA

Le Nozze di Figaro
Cherubino

The Turn of the Screw
Governess

Don Pasquale
Norina

Il Barbiere di Siviglia
Rosina

ROLES STUDIED

Rigoletto
Gilda

Cosi fan Tutte
Dorabella

Ariadne auf Naxos
Zerbinetta

L'Egisto
Amor

TRAINING

Boston Conservatory of Music, B.M., 2002
Voice: Elaine Grissell, David Corson
Master Classes: Mari Martin, Jan DeGreux, Robert Capon

AWARDS/FESTIVALS

Finalist, Regional Metropolitan Opera Auditions, 2001
Tanglewood Music Festival, 2002
Aspen Music Festival, 2001

Chapter 6

Sample Cover Letters

This chapter contains sample cover letters for people pursuing a wide variety of jobs and careers in the performing arts, or who already have experience in this field.

There are many different styles of cover letters in terms of layout, level of formality, and presentation of information. These samples also represent people with varying amounts of education and work experience. Choose one cover letter or borrow elements from several different cover letters to help you construct your own.

—————— **Kenneth M. Shannon** ——————
flute

School Address   **Home Address**
Marks Hall, Room 224   45 Long Avenue
University of Colorado   Arlington, VA 22202
Boulder, CO 80310   (703) 555-3574
(303) 555-3120

February 1, 20--

Don Sullivan, Director
Richmond Summer Institute
545 N. Seaview
Richmond, VA 22031

Dear Mr. Sullivan:

Please accept my resume as a precursor to the application process for the
Summer Institute.

I am currently studying flute performance at the Boulder School of Music,
University of Colorado. I feel that your intensive program that combines
orchestral performance with chamber and repertory classes is exactly what
I need to continue my education during my summer break. I will be applying
for a scholarship if accepted to audition, but am aware that this has no bearing
on your decision. As a native of Virginia, I am very excited at the prospect of
working with you at the institute.

Thank you very much for your time. I look forward to hearing from you soon.

With regards,

Kenneth M. Shannon

Derrick Johnson, Bass

245 N. Abbott Dr.
Bloomington, IN 46802
812-555-6144

September 10, 20--

Bel Canto Foundation
P.O. Box 652
Wilmette, IL 60625

Dear Competition Coordinator:

I am a bassist pursuing my degree in performance at Indiana University. I am interested in auditioning to compete in the junior division (ages 18–22) of your upcoming competition. I understand that I will be competing in the Midwest region if my application is accepted.

Please send me an application and any other materials necessary to complete this process. I have enclosed my resume in advance for your information and consideration.

I look forward to hearing from you soon.

Sincerely,

Derrick Johnson

Beatrice Young   *Mezzo-Soprano*

4501 West Mill Road • Grosse Pointe, MI 48072
B.Young@xxx.com • 313/555-1234

May 12, 20--

Greater Michigan Opera Theater
8922 Three Pines Road
Lansing, MI 44026

To Whom It May Concern:

I am a mezzo-soprano with a master's degree in voice from the University of Michigan. I am seeking opportunities in young artist programs, and your company is of great interest to me. As a resident of Michigan, I am very familiar with the Opera Theater and would love the opportunity to work with you in future seasons.

This season I was a finalist in the Metropolitan Opera Auditions, Great Lakes District. Recent solo highlights include performances with the Detroit Symphony and the Windham Chorale. My diverse operatic repertoire includes Mercedes in *Carmen*, Second Lady in *The Magic Flute*, and Mother in *Amahl and the Night Visitors*.

I would like to request any information you have regarding the Young Artist Opera Theater Program, and I have included a self-addressed envelope. I am currently available to audition at any time. Thank you for your time and consideration and I eagerly look forward to hearing from you.

Sincerely,

Beatrice Young

MARIA GONZALEZ
Double Bass

Home Address
2565 Cooper Avenue
San Francisco, CA 93120
613-555-4788

School Address
114 East 23rd Street #16B
New York, NY 10018
212-555-0213

November 15, 20--

Eugene Bibbs
Personnel Director
San Diego Philharmonic
San Diego, CA 93188

Dear Mr. Bibbs:

I am writing in regard to an audition for the position of assistant principal double bass with the San Diego Philharmonic Orchestra. My performance degree is from the Juilliard School of Music, where I currently study with Vaughan Chambers. I will receive my degree this coming May, at which time I am planning to return to the West Coast.

My performance experience includes the following:

- San Francisco Symphony Orchestra, 2001
- Greenwich Symphony Orchestra: Principal, 2000-present
- Mt. Vernon Chamber Players, 1998-2000
- Juilliard Chamber Orchestra: Principal, 2001-present
- Juilliard Contemporary Ensemble: Assistant Principal, 1999-present
- Juilliard Orchestra: Assistant Principal, 1998-present

Earlier this year I was one of three finalists for the principal double bass position with the Dayton Symphony. I am a former student of Robert Pytorski, principal with the San Francisco Symphony, and continue to have lessons with him when I return to the Bay Area.

Please send me your audition schedule and a list of repertoire for the season. Thank you for your time and consideration.

Sincerely,

Maria Gonzalez

Michael Alan Pierce
french horn

145 Main Street #2
Bangor, ME 04322
(207) 555-3236
MAPierce@xxx.com

June 15, 20--

Dr. Ariel Blumfield
Admissions Director
New England College of Music
330 Columbus Avenue
Boston, MA 02115

Dear Dr. Blumfield:

I am a recent college graduate with a bachelor's degree in french horn performance from the Peabody Conservatory of Music. I am planning to return to the New England area to begin seeking my graduate degree, and I am greatly interested in your school. As indicated by my resume, I have extensive performance experience and I'm a member of several musical organizations.

I am currently studying with Donna Burke, who is on your adjunct faculty for the upcoming year. I would continue to study with her if I were accepted into the program. Please also feel free to contact Ms. Burke at (207) 555-7878 for further reference.

If you could please send me any information you may have regarding your graduate performance program, it would be greatly appreciated. Thank you very much for your time. I look forward to hearing from you soon.

Sincerely,

Michael Alan Pierce

Martha Oki, Oboe

68447 Oahu Drive
Honolulu, Hawaii 96732
808-555-4700
M.Oki@xxx.com

April 30, 20--

Audition Committee
Cleveland Orchestra
P.O. Box 2657
Cleveland, OH 44025

To whom it may concern:

I am interested in the position of Principal Oboe with the Cleveland Orchestra. As a player with experience in orchestras throughout the country, I feel I would be an asset to the section. I have enclosed my resume for your consideration, and I would be happy to provide any references you might require for the invitation to audition.

Thank you for your time. I look forward to hearing from you.

Sincerely,

Martha Oki

CARY T. CHRISTIAN

24 Pawnee Valley Road • Brockport, NY 14420
CTChristian@xxx.com • 716-555-8102

March 30, 20--

Dr. Alan Hessman
Jefferson Public Academy
111 N. Dobson Blvd.
White Plains, NY 12461

Dear Dr. Hessman,

I thoroughly enjoyed our telephone conversation on March 26th. Per our conversation, I have enclosed the resume you requested. As you may remember, I am anticipating graduation in May with my B.A. in Education and Organ Performance from Eastman School of Music and I'm seeking a teaching position in your middle school. With ten years of experience teaching at the elementary, high school, and university level, I feel prepared to enter the public school sector as a skilled and qualified teacher.

The enclosed resume highlights my teaching experience and conducting positions at the School of Music. In addition to these duties, I was deeply involved in the Rochester School District. I feel strongly that music plays an integral part in a child's development, and I believe I can promote an understanding and love of music that is sorely needed in the public school system.

I commend you and your school on such fine work in this and many other areas to date. I would like to become a part of such essential work in the future.

I look forward to hearing from you.

Sincerely,

Cary T. Christian

Sarah J. Lindenbaum

Home Address
152 North Avenue
Wilmette, IL 60122
(847) 555-3388

School Address
33 Maple Avenue
Ann Arbor, MI 49023
(413) 555-6672

May 1, 20--

Beatrice Russell, Principal
Andrews Academy
Freeport, Connecticut 05845

Dear Ms. Russell,

As a 1989 graduate with a Bachelor of Music Education from the University of Michigan School of Music, I am interested in being a member of the faculty of Andrews Academy.

My interest in Andrews Academy is in part due to its strong commitment to giving a high quality education to "high risk" children. The progressive and innovative philosophy of encouraging such students to reach their full potential through musical expression proves the school's dedication to the arts.

The enclosed resume highlights both my performance experience and teaching credentials. My experiences as a lecturer have included historical performance classes with special emphasis on the Renaissance period. I have taught cello in the Ann Arbor Public School System as well as at the university level. In addition to teaching, I have coached chamber music at all levels of ability. I feel my extracurricular interest and skills in singing and dance also are an asset for any successful teacher. I have the needed energy, cooperative spirit, dedication, and skills to make a positive contribution to your school.

Although I am not currently enrolled in school, I am prepared to enter a master's program in conjunction with the position, if this is desired. Please instruct me on how I should proceed. I will be returning to Connecticut in July, but will be available to interview by telephone until that time. Thank you so much for your time and consideration.

Sincerely,

Sarah J. Lindenbaum

Elizabeth Moss, Soprano

2347 N. Oak St. • Lake Forest, IL 60604
Beth.Moss@xxx.com • (847) 555-5010

September 1, 20--

Toledo Opera Theater
P.O. Box 39270
Toledo, OH 44023

Toledo Opera Theater:

Please accept the enclosed resume and photos for your files. I am seeking opportunities as a principal or chorus member and would appreciate receiving your audition schedule or any information you have in that regard. I look forward to hearing from you at your convenience.

Sincerely,

Elizabeth Moss

Enclosures: resume/photo

MARTIN ALONZO

525 N. Oaktree Dr.
Seattle, WA 55020
(704) 555-6683
M.Alonzo@xxx.com

Tenor
Hair: Black
Height: 6'2"
Eyes: Brown

September 16, 20--

To Whom It May Concern:

I am sending the enclosed resume for your consideration. As illustrated by my resume, I am a versatile and energetic performer with extensive experience in opera, operetta, concert, and theater, specializing in original works. I am seeking to further expand my portfolio and would appreciate any information you may have regarding auditions with your company.

Thank you for your time and effort. I look forward to hearing from you.

Sincerely,

Martin Alonzo

Stanley Beltzman

Trumpet

22 Ridge Avenue • Lexington, MA 02113
S.Beltzman@xxx.com • (617) 555-3212

September 15, 20--

Mrs. Najera Roe
Auditions Committee Coordinator
Boston Symphony Orchestra
One Massachusetts Avenue
Boston, MA 02115

Dear Mrs. Roe:

I am a recent graduate of New England Conservatory with a master's degree with honors in performance. I am interested in taking your upcoming audition for substitute principal trumpet. I am currently studying with Rudolph Blintz and am sending my resume upon his recommendation. I am aware that the audition process is very selective, but I trust that you will give my credentials fair consideration. Needless to say, it would be an honor to play for your committee.

If you have any questions or require further recommendations, please feel free to contact me at your convenience. I greatly look forward to hearing from you.

Sincerely,

Stanley Beltzman

Enclosure: resume

barry kim   actor/singer

16 Brookfield Road • Hartford, CT 07450
(203) 555-7879 • B.Kim@xxx.com

March 22, 20--

Mrs. Jeannie Hartman, Director
Rosewood Summer Theater
10 The Woodlands
Rosewood, VT 05660

Dear Mrs. Hartman,

I am currently a junior at the Ethel Barrymore High School for the Performing Arts in LaFayette, New York. I am writing to obtain information regarding your theater company and am interested primarily in performance opportunities.

Although I have never been employed by a theater company, I have attended the Hartt Performance Center for Young Artists for five consecutive summers in addition to adhering to the rigorous schedule and curriculum of the High School for the Performing Arts during the school year.

As my resume indicates, I have had training in acting, singing, dance, and stage combat as well as piano. My recent performance credits include the title role in *The King and I* at the high school and an appearance as a soloist in Bernstein's *Chichester Psalms* at Mount Sinai Temple in LaFayette, for which I received a favorable mention in the *LaFayette Gazette*.

I believe a position with your company would be excellent preparation for a performing arts career. Thank you in advance for your time.

Yours sincerely,

Barry Kim

Beverly Whitfield
61 Sanders Avenue, #302
New Haven, CT 07450
(203) 555-1644
B.Whitfield@xxx.com

April 1, 20--

Newcastle Summer Theater
P.O. Box 250
Newcastle, Maine 04030

Dear Newcastle Summer Theater:

I am writing to inquire about your summer theater program. I am an actress completing a degree in English with an emphasis in Theater. As indicated by the enclosed resume, however, my extracurricular stage experience is extensive and greatly served to enhance my academic endeavors.

Although I am primarily seeking to expand my acting portfolio, I am interested in your technical program as well. Please send me any information you have in regard to both programs, or contact me at the above number. Thank you for your time, and I look forward to hearing from you soon.

Cordially,

Beverly Whitfield

ELIA M. GREY   **Capri Artists Ltd.**
Comedian/Actor   130 W. 10th St., Suite 302
AFTRA   New York, NY 10012
                                        (212) 555-5434

Lana Barnes Mitchell, Casting
The Elaine Stevens Show
25 Rockefeller Plaza, Suite 1010
New York, NY 10122

Dear Ms. Mitchell,

I am a working actress and stand-up comedienne, and I would like to be considered for work on "The Elaine Stevens Show." Under fives and extra work would always be a wonderful addition to my expanding resume. I believe it's the best show on television, and I feel that I could be a perfect fit with the cast.

Thank you for your time and consideration. I look forward to having the opportunity to audition for you soon.

Sincerely,

Elia M. Grey

------- MICHAEL DODGE -------
------ 18 CRESTWELL LANE ------
---- DUBUQUE, IA 52008 ----
---- 312-555-0980 ----

June 10, 20--

Ms. Patricia Dobson-Hull
Assistant Director of Marketing
Iowa State Opera
One Grace Plaza
Ames, IA 53221

Dear Ms. Dobson-Hull:

I am writing to follow up on our conversation of June 5th. As you may recall, I am a graduate of Grinnell College interested in the position of public relations assistant in your marketing department.

As we discussed, I am enclosing my resume for your consideration. I believe that a small but growing company such as yours would be the perfect place for me to build upon my skills in the field of arts management. I feel that my varied work experience as an admissions assistant at Grinnell, in addition to work with the Iowa Symphony and extracurricular performance activities, should further indicate my suitability for the position.

Please contact me at the above address to schedule an interview. I greatly enjoyed talking to you and look forward to hearing from you again soon.

Sincerely,

Michael Dodge

Sandy Johnson
845 Windy Lane
Springfield, MO 65802
314-555-0980

July 15, 20--

Mr. Jim Lee
2828 N. Pine Grove
Chicago, IL 60657

Dear Mr. Lee:

I am a recent graduate of Washington University with a bachelor's degree in music, and I am looking for a position in arts management. Jan Vitner, a career placement counselor at Washington, thought that you might be a good lead to any possibilities in the field in the Chicago area. I will be moving to the area in September and hope to secure employment by that time.

I have enclosed a resume for your reference. If you know of anyone who is in need of talents like mine in the near future, please let me know, or feel free to pass on my resume. Any assistance you can offer in this regard would be greatly appreciated.

In any event, I am interested in any suggestions you may have for a recent graduate with performance and management skills going out into the "real world." Please let me know if I may call you when I am in Chicago next month. I would like to discuss these matters further at your convenience. I look forward to meeting you.

Sincerely,

Sandy Johnson

Tammy Baker
432 Ohio Avenue
Fort Worth, TX 76038
817-555-5478

September 20, 20--

Mrs. Marsha Ames Wallace
Silver Spring School of Dance
10 Shady Tree Road
Silver Spring, MD 20901

Dear Mrs. Wallace,

In December, I will graduate from Texas Christian University with a B.F.A. in dance, and I am seeking part-time teaching opportunities. Having received a scholarship to attend the Silver Spring School in the summer of 1994, and remembering that experience with great fondness, I immediately thought to write and update you as to my progress.

In the past four years I have received extensive training and have gained substantial performance experience as a dancer, with most attention to ballet and modern. In addition to the required courses, I have done supplementary work in jazz and tap at the Rosario Dance Studio, where I am also currently a teacher. Additional teaching experience includes two years at Dance Dallas, where I teach ballet and jazz. For the last three years I have concurrently maintained a small private studio under the auspices of the university.

My early experiences at the Silver Spring School and the Dallas School of the Arts contributed greatly to my love of dance and continue to fuel my desire to teach. I have included my resume for your reference. I am interested in any positions available at the beginning of next year. Thank you for your time and consideration.

Sincerely yours,

Tammy Baker

Ginny Rae Bell
Comedienne

P.O. Box 2282   **GinnyBell@xxx.com**
San Jose, CA 95125   **510-555-7382**

January 22, 20--

Nicole Gerson, Casting Director
Comedy Acts Live
Comedy Central
40 Rockefeller Center
New York, NY 10122

Dear Ms. Gerson,

I am an energetic and creative comedienne who would very much like to be a part of Comedy Acts Live. I have been watching the show since it began and believe that my versatile talents would be a perfect fit with the show's unique brand of humor.

I am interested in either writing or performing on the show, but will accept anything that is available in order to be a part of what I believe to be the funniest half-hour on television. I have been living in the San Jose area but would be happy to relocate if a position were available.

I am enclosing a recent head shot and resume for your consideration. Most recently, I have produced a comedy showcase at the House of Comedy in Berkeley, which is scheduled to run again this spring. Please come and catch the show if you're ever in the Bay Area.

I thank you for your time and hope to have the pleasure of meeting you soon.

Sincerely,

Ginny Rae Bell

DANICA HARRIS

Coloratura Soprano
508 9th Street • Brooklyn, NY 11215 • (718) 555-3735

April 3, 20--

Ms. Shari Engel
President, Concert Artists New York
220 Lexington Avenue
New York, NY 10022

Dear Ms. Engel:

It was a great pleasure listening to your lecture and talking with you at the singer's workshop at the Brooklyn College today. I feel inspired by your successful career as an agent and businesswoman and the energy and drive that led you to that success. I plan to follow the advice you gave me regarding my materials and contacting the people you had mentioned. Thank you for the wonderful tips. I will keep you informed of my progress. I hope to have the pleasure of working with you in the future.

Yours sincerely,

Danica Harris

Laralynn Jennings
234 Mapletree Avenue
Baltimore, MD 21216
410-555-5478

After December 15th:
14 Monarch Drive
Takoma Park, MD 20911
(301) 555-6954

September 20, 20--

Babette Lyons, Editor
Dance Art Magazine
1000 9th Street
Washington, DC 20015

Dear Ms. Lyons,

In December 2004, I will be a graduate of the University of Maryland with a B.F.A. in dance. I am seeking a position at any level in the dance field, preferably as a performer, but I am also seeking part-time teaching opportunities. Mira Browning, my advisor and teacher, recommended that I contact you for information concerning job opportunities in the field. I am interested specifically in positions available at the beginning of next year.

In the past four years I have received extensive training and have gained substantial performance experience as a dancer, with most attention to ballet and modern. In addition to the required courses, I have done supplementary work in jazz and tap at the Brighton Dance Studio, where I also teach.

Additional teaching experience includes two years at Dance Baltimore, where I teach ballet and jazz to children and adults.

I would appreciate any information concerning available positions, or names and addresses of other people whom I could contact. If it would be more convenient, I would be glad to call you. Please let me know when and where it is best to reach you.

Sincerely yours,

Laralynn Jennings